THE BIG ROYAL QUIZ BOOK

THE BIG ROYAL QUIZ BOOK

John Van der Kiste

A & F Publications

First published 2014
Second edition 2016
© 2014, 2016 John Van der Kiste
All rights reserved

A & F Publications
South Brent, Devon,
England, UK
Printed by CreateSpace

Typeset 11pt Georgia

ISBN-13: 978-1530734054
ISBN-10: 1530734053

CONTENTS

Introduction   4
1. Lucky Dip   7
2. Browsing in the biographies   10
3. So here it is, Royal Christmas, everybody's having fun   11
4. Music   13
5. Nicknames   15
6. Death or glory – but certainly death   16
7. An assassination has been announced   17
8. Good book, Your Majesty (or Your Highness)   18
9. Treading the boards   19
10. Palaces, Residences and Abbeys   20
11. The truth, the whole truth – or maybe not   21
12. Lucky Dip 2   23
13. Royal food   26
14. A bit on the side   29
15. Now for the novels and plays   30
16. Go on, quote me   32
17. Dates, dates and more dates   34
18. Yes, Prime Minister   36

19. Dogs and other pets   37
20. A royal musical free-for-all   39
21. Abdications   41
22. Lucky Dip 3   42
23. Armed forces   45
24. Who and who, or whom, or what   47
25. The big picture   49
26. Another quotation round   51
27. Politicians   53
28. A question of sport   55
29. Bagehot   57
30. Shakespeare   59
31. 1066 And All That   62
32. Farjeon's Kings and Queens   64
33. Lucky Dip 4   66
34. The Normans   69
35. The Plantagenets   71
36. The Lancastrians   73
37. The Yorkists   75
38. King Henry VII   77
39. King Henry VIII   79
40. King Edward VI and Queen Mary I   81
41. Queen Elizabeth I   83
42. King James I and King Charles I   85
43. King Charles II and King James II   87
44. King William III, Queen Mary II and Queen Anne   89
45. King George I   91
46. King George II   93
47. King George III   95
48. King George IV   97

49. King William IV 99
50. Queen Victoria 101
51. King Edward VII 103
52. Queen Victoria's children 105
53. King George V 107
54. King Edward VIII 109
55. King George VI 111
56. Queen Elizabeth II 113
57. Scottish Kings and Queens 115
58. European Kings and Emperors 117
59 Kings of France 119
60. The Romanovs 121
61. Emperor Francis Joseph 123
62. Emperor William II 125
63. The Battenbergs and Mountbattens 127
64. Who's on the cover? 129
65. Lucky Dip 5 130

Answers 133

INTRODUCTION

While discussing possibilities for forthcoming projects one morning at home, as you do, my wife Kim suggested I ought to think about compiling a royal quiz book. At once the ideas for topics and individual questions started presenting themselves thick and fast, and for much of the day she found it quite difficult to prise me away from my laptop and my books. (She only had herself to blame...) After a few months of discussion, exchanging of further ideas, research, trawling my personal library and checking many websites, here is the result.

As several other royal quiz books published in recent years have focused almost exclusively on British royalty, either on the present royal family or on a Kings and Queens approach, I have not only covered these but also gone back very briefly to the pre-Norman conquest era. I have also placed some emphasis on European monarchs and their families from the medieval age to the present day as well. In addition to these, the occasional question about the Brazilian, Egyptian and Thailand monarchies, even the odd Roman Emperor (arguably not royal, but there you go), has found its way in.

As ever, the compiler of quizzes, be they for books or the pub, is faced with the dilemma of how easy or hard the questions ought to be. Of course, they're all easy – if you know the answer. I have aimed for a balance, hoping not to put users off by making them too insultingly simple on the one hand, or too devastatingly specialist on the other.

And, if in doubt, just make a guess at the answer and you could be right. There is also, I hope, an assortment of serious and entertaining material. Some of it, particularly in the music sections, may be a little on the tenuous side. Elsewhere, particularly in the questions relating to monarchs who reigned more than two or three centuries ago, these may relate more to events during their reigns, such as battles, treaties, places and the like, than to their personal lives, details of which are often lacking, lost in the mists of time.

But basically, the idea is to have fun – and perhaps learn a little along the way. You have 850 questions, more or less, and 65 rounds on a variety of themes. There are five 'Lucky Dips' of 25 questions each at intervals, and several batches of 12 on assorted subjects. OK...enjoy!

In conclusion, many thanks to Kim, who not only came up with the idea and continually encouraged me, but also provided several suggestions for topics and helped to think up questions for some of the categories as well. To some extent this is thus a joint effort.

The first edition was published in 2014. This second has been redesigned to a major extent, updated, and several new rounds, comprising over a hundred new questions, have been added.

John Van der Kiste
March 2016

QUESTIONS

1. Lucky Dip

Here are twenty-five general royalty questions all designed to ease you in gently. Most of these are pretty easy, but rest assured this will not necessarily be a taste of things to come further on. Unless stated otherwise, assume that all Kings and Queens are of England.

1. Which is the Queen's official London residence? *Buckingham Palace*
2. Which King of England had the longest reign? *George III*
3. Which one of Henry VIII's wives survived him? *Catherine Parr*
4. Which King was killed while he was hunting in the New Forest? *William II*
5. Which King reigned jointly with his wife and Queen for five years, and after her death, on his own for the remaining seven until his death? *William III*
6. Which King led his troops to victory at the battle of Agincourt? *Henry V*
7. The Romanovs ruled over which empire? *Russia*
8. What was the family name of Queen Elizabeth the Queen Mother? *Bowes-Lyon*

9. Which King was deposed, imprisoned and put to death at Berkeley Castle, according to tradition, by a red-hot poker being thrust somewhere very unpleasant?

10. Which Roman Emperor is said to have fiddled while Rome burned?

11. Which King lost the crown jewels in the Wash?

12. Who is supposed to have said, 'If they have no bread, let them eat cake'?

13. Which King was executed at Whitehall on 30 January 1649?

14. Which King was killed while besieging a castle in Aquitaine in 1199?

15. Who was the only sovereign to have been crowned King of England and France?

16. Which Queen regnant married King Philip II of Spain?

17. Who was the only King of Great Britain to have been buried at Hanover?

18. Which dukedom links King Richard III and Prince Henry, the third son of King George V?

19. Which King of Spain left his country when the monarchy went into abeyance in 1931?

20. Which King completely rebuilt Westminster Abbey in the 13th century?

21. What was the name of Queen Elizabeth II's yacht, decommissioned in 1997?

22. During whose reign was Calais, England's last possession, lost to the French?

23. Who was the first of Queen Elizabeth II's Prime Ministers to be born after her accession?

24. Which King married the widow of his elder brother?

25. In which month and year did Queen Elizabeth II overtake Queen Victoria's record of 63 years on the throne to become the longest-reigning British monarch?

2. Browsing in the biographies

The following titles are biographies of which royal figures? To help you a little, the answers are in chronological order of birth of each subject.

1. *England's black legend*, Desmond Seward
2. *Love and the princess*, Lucille Iremonger
3. *The Royal George*, Giles St Aubyn
4. *King without a crown*, Daphne Bennett
5. *The lonely Empress*, Joan Haslip
6. *Unpredictable Queen*, E.E.P. Tisdall
7. *The dream King*, Wilfrid Blunt
8. *A Habsburg tragedy*, Judith Listowel
9. *An unbroken unity*, E.M. Almedingen
10. *The last romantic*, Hannah Pakula
11. *The last princess*, Matthew Dennison
12. *No ordinary crown*, Stelio Hourmouzios

3. So here it is, Royal Christmas, everybody's having fun

We wish you a royal Christmas with these festive questions:

1. Which King was crowned on Christmas Day at Westminster Abbey?
2. Before Prince Albert, which member of the royal family generally had a yew tree every year as part of the Christmas decorations?
3. In which year did King George V make his first Christmas broadcast on the BBC?
4. Which well-known author and journalist of the time co-wrote the broadcast referred to in the above question, with the King (and coincidentally predeceased the King by two days)?
5. Which member of the royal family was born on Christmas Day 1936?
6. Where did Queen Victoria generally spend Christmas throughout most of her adult life?
7. Who wrote the poem 'God knows', more popularly known as 'The gate of the year', from which King George VI quoted in his 1939 Christmas broadcast?
8. Where do the British royal family generally spend Christmas? Sandringham

9. In which year did Queen Elizabeth II make the first televised Christmas broadcast?

10. Which play was written by Shakespeare, probably around 1601-2, as an entertainment for the close of the Christmas season?

11. Which future King was born at Beaumont Palace, Oxford, on Christmas Eve 1167?

12. What was stolen by Glaswegian students from Westminster Abbey on Christmas Day 1950?

4. Music

How well do you know your classical and popular music royal connections?

1. Which German composer dedicated his *Scottish Symphony* to Queen Victoria?
2. Who sang a rewritten version of his song *Candle in the Wind* at the funeral service for Princess Diana in September 1997?
3. Which group played in front of the Prince of Wales at Birmingham National Exhibition Centre in May 1982, the first rock concert attended by an immediate member of the Queen's family ([although other British royalty, not quite so close to the Queen, had already done so – see 10 below]?
4. Which group named themselves after an ill-fated Austrian Archduke and heir of the early 20th century?
5. Which guitarist played the National Anthem on the roof of Buckingham Palace at the start of the Golden Jubilee pop concert in 2002?
6. Which of the Beatles said onstage at the Royal Variety Performance in 1963: 'For our last number I'd like to ask your help. The people in the cheaper seats clap your hands, and the rest of you, if you'd just rattle your jewellery'?
7. For whose funeral did Purcell compose a March, Canzone and Anthem in 1695?

8. Which composer, a great favourite of Queen Victoria, was knighted by her in 1883?

9. In the Grand Knockout Tournament, often known as It's A Royal Knockout, shown on BBC TV in June 1987, whose team included Eddy Grant, Tom Jones and Sheena Easton?

10. Which group performed a charity concert at the Wembley Empire Pool, in June 1978, in the presence of the Duke and Duchess of Gloucester?

11. Handel's *Music for the Royal Fireworks* was composed under contract for King George II in 1749 to celebrate the end of the War of the Austrian Succession and the signing of which treaty?

12. Which instrument was played by Alfred, Duke of Edinburgh, who sometimes performed on it in symphony orchestras?

5. Nicknames

Which royalties, all crowned heads or consorts, were sometimes known or are best remembered by the following nicknames?

1. Harefoot
2. Curtmantle
3. Lionheart
4. Lackland
5. The Hammer of the Scots
6. Crookback Dick
7. Bluff King Hal
8. The Flanders mare
9. Old Rowley
10. The Sun King
11. The First Gentleman in Europe
12. Tum-Tum

6. Death or glory – well, certainly death

Can you name the main royal casualties who fell at these battles or sieges?

1. Watling Street, 61
2. Adrianople, 378
3. Soissons, 923
4. Clontarf, 1014
5. Stamford Bridge, 1066
6. Hastings, 1066
7. Velbazhd, 1330
8. Crecy, 1346
9. Bosworth, 1485
10. Sauchieburn, 1488
11. Flodden Field, 1513
12. Halden, 1718

7. An assassination has been announced

Which European crowned heads or senior royals were assassinated at the following places in these years?

1. Delft, 1584
2. Paris, 1589
3. Paris, 1610
4. Stockholm, 1792
5. St Petersburg, 1881
6. Geneva, 1898
7. Monza, 1900
8. Belgrade, 1903
9. Lisbon, 1908
10. Salonika, 1913
11. Sarajevo, 1914
12. Marseille, 1934

8. Good book, Your Majesty (or Your Highness)

Which royal personages wrote or edited the following books, all listed in chronological order of date of publication?

1. *Defence of the Seven Sacraments* (1521)
2. *My ancestors* (1929)
3. *I was to be Empress* (1937)
4. *In Napoleonic Days* (1941)
5. *My memories of six reigns* (1956)
6. *For a King's love* (1956)
7. *The heart has its reasons* (1956)
8. *The old man of Lochnagar* (1980)
9. *The tongs and the bones* (1981)
10. *Men, Machines and Sacred Cows* (1984)
11. *Crowned in a far country* (1986)
12. *Budgie the little helicopter* (1989)

9. Treading the boards

Which crowned heads or senior royals have been portrayed on stage or screen (film and TV) by the following actors and actresses? Again, the names of the answers are given in chronological order of birth:

1. Keith Michell, Charles Laughton, Robert Shaw
2. Flora Robson, Bette Davis, Glenda Jackson
3. Nigel Davenport, Nigel Hawthorne, Alex Jennings
4. Peter Ustinov, Peter Egan, Rupert Everett
5. Prunella Scales, Anna Neagle, Annette Crosbie
6. Anton Walbrook, Frank Thornton, Robert Hardy
7. Gemma Jones, Felicity Kendal, Zizi Strallen
8. Timothy West, Derek Francis, Thorley Walters
9. Barry Foster, Christopher Neame, Rainer Sellien
10. Michael Gambon, Marius Goring, Tom Hollander
11. Michael Jayston, Charles Kay, Michael Billington
12. Colin Firth, Andrew Ray, James Wilby

19

10. Palaces, Residences and Abbeys

1. Which King commissioned the building of the Royal Pavilion, Brighton?
2. In which French abbey are King Henry II and King Richard I buried?
3. Which palace was once known as the King's House, Pimlico?
4. Who was the last King to live at Hampton Court Palace?
5. Which Scottish palace was burned down during an accidental fire in 1746?
6. For whom was Sandringham originally purchased in 1861?
7. To which palace did the French royal family move from Versailles shortly after the outbreak of the French revolution in 1789?
8. Which palace was gutted by fire in 1497 but rebuilt by King Henry VII?
9. At which British royal home is there a Swiss Cottage in the gardens?
10. Who constructed Queen Mary's dolls' house?
11. Where did King Edward VIII sign his act of abdication?
12. At which palace in the Crimea did Tsar Alexander III die in 1894, and the Yalta conference of 1945 at the end of the Second World War take place?

11. The truth, the whole truth – or maybe not

Are these statements true or false? There are six of each – and 'partly true, partly false' counts as false.

1. Queen Victoria and Prince Albert had 42 grandchildren, of whom 34 survived to adulthood.
2. The body of Maximilian, Emperor of Mexico, who was executed by firing squad in 1867, was buried in Mexico in accordance with instructions he had left shortly before he was captured.
3. In addition to four disgraced former Members of Parliament in the late twentieth century, the only person who is known to have voluntarily resigned membership of the Privy Council – and the only royal person - was Queen Victoria's second son Prince Alfred, Duke of Edinburgh, after he became Duke of Saxe-Coburg Gotha.
4. Prince Joachim, youngest son of German Emperor William II, was suggested by Irish politicians at the time of the Easter Rising in 1916 as a possible King of independent Ireland.
5. King Charles II was the last Catholic King of England.

6. King George III's only visit overseas was to Ireland.

7. Edward Lear, famous for his limericks and watercolour paintings, was once Queen Victoria's art master.

8. While Prince and Princess of Wales, King Edward VII and Queen Alexandra narrowly escaped assassination at the hands of an anarchist while they were on a visit to Berlin.

9. Queen Elizabeth the Queen Mother died in 2002 at the age of 101, an age never surpassed before or since by any other member of the British royal family.

10. Richard II is allegedly the first British King ever to use a pocket handkerchief.

11. When Edward the Confessor was crowned at Winchester Cathedral in 1043, it was the last English coronation ever to be held outside Westminster Abbey.

12. King George IV's estranged wife Queen Caroline insisted on being admitted to his coronation at Westminster Abbey, and was only grudgingly let in when she threatened to bring a contingent of soldiers to help her enter by force.

12. Lucky Dip 2

A little more demanding than the opening round, perhaps.

1. Who was the only sovereign to be crowned King of England and France?
2. Prime Minister David Cameron is descended from which British sovereign?
3. Prince Leopold of Saxe-Coburg married Princess Charlotte of Wales who died in childbirth, and was later proclaimed King of which European kingdom?
4. Who was born on Malta in 1876?
5. Which overseas territory issued a set of postage stamps in 1911 commemorating the coronation of King George V, with individual portraits of several members of the royal family who have rarely (and in the case of the King's youngest son, never) been shown on stamps before or since?
6. Who wrote 'There is no necessity to separate the monarch from the mob; all authority is equally bad'?
7. King Philip IV and Queen Mariana of Spain can be seen in the image of the mirror above the artist's head in the painting *Las Meniñas* (The Maids of Honour), but who was the artist?
8. Which Queen Consort was buried in 1291 at the Abbey of St Mary and St Melor, Amesbury?

9. In the twelfth century, which English King also held the title Count of Boulogne?

10. Which European monarch was seriously embarrassed by his so-called interview published in the *Daily Telegraph* in October 1908?

11. In which city were the remains of King Richard III discovered in 2012, and laid to rest in the cathedral in March 2015?

12. Which King's favourite at court was Piers Gaveston?

13. When she was brought the news in 1952 of the death of her father King George VI, Queen Elizabeth II was at Treetops Game Reserve, in which country?

14. To which royal house do the princes of Monaco belong?

15. Who was said to have been drowned in a butt of Malmsey wine in the tower of London in 1478?

16. Under the pseudonym Ingahild Grathmer, Queen Margrethe of Denmark's illustrations were used in the Danish edition published in 1977 of which famous English work of literature?

17. Although he died at the age of eleven in 1700, who was the longest-lived child of Queen Anne?

18. Who was King of England from 1016 to 1035, and throughout most of those years also King of Denmark?

19. Which European country was reigned over only by women throughout the twentieth century?

20. Who was born on Corfu in 1921?

21. When King Louis XIV of France died in 1715, he was succeeded by Louis XV, who was

aged five. What relation was the boy King to his predecessor? *Grandson*

22. Which Greek King did Aspasia Manos marry in a secret ceremony in November 1919? *Constantine. Ij Alexander*

23. Princess Marie of Edinburgh, granddaughter of Queen Victoria, married which future European King in 1893? *Prince Ferdinand of Romania*

24. Which future British King served in the West Indies under the command of Admiral Nelson? *William IV*

Lord Darnley
25. Who was murdered at Kirk o'Field, Edinburgh, in February 1567?

13. Royal food

Whet your appetite with these culinary questions. You can always go and raid the kitchen later.

1. Which cake, which usually consisted of raspberry jam and whipped double cream or vanilla cream sandwiched between two sponge cakes, the top one generally decorated with a dusting of icing sugar, was named after the monarch who was said to enjoy a slice with her afternoon tea?
2. Which combination including cooked cold chicken meat, raisins, herbs, spices and a creamy mayonnaise-based sauce which can be eaten either as a salad or used as sandwich filling, and sometimes flavoured with curry powder or paste, was invented for a special occasion by Constance Spry and Rosemary Hume from the Cordon Bleu Cookery School in London?
3. In the sixteenth century, who would use a peacock feather to make herself vomit between courses in order to create space for more food?
4. In 1874, the London bakery Peek Freans introduced the Marie Biscuit to commemorate whose wedding?
5. Which potato was developed by John Butler of Scotter, Lincolnshire, and given a

royal name in honour of a major event taking place that same year?

6. The Margherita Pizza was first made in 1889 by the Neapolitan cook Raffaele Esposito, according to tradition to mark a visit by whom? *Queen of Spain (Isabella)*

7. Crepe Suzette is a French dessert said to have been created in 1895 at Monte Carlo for a visiting senior member of royalty and his guest Suzette, in whose honour he asked for the dish to be named; who was the royal? *Ed VII*

8. Queen Elizabeth the Queen Mother was particularly partial to a tipple containing a slice of lemon and a mixture of which two alcoholic beverages? *Gin*

9. Which light sponge cake with the pieces in a distinctive pink and yellow check pattern, held together by strawberry jam and covered in marzipan, is said to have been made first for the wedding of Princess Victoria of Hesse and the Rhine and Prince Louis in 1884, and named after the German town from which the bridegroom and his brothers took their family name?

10. According to the Duke of Wellington, who was Prime Minister at the time, on 9 April 1830 who ate a breakfast consisting of a pigeon and beefsteak pie, washed down by 'three parts of a bottle of Mozelle, a glass of champagne, two glasses of port, followed by a glass of brandy'?

11. With which supermarket chain did Duchy Originals, a company which launched a brand of organic food set up by Charles, Prince of Wales in 1990, sign an exclusive deal to originate, manufacture, distribute and sell Duchy products within the United Kingdom? *Waitrose*

12. Who was Queen Victoria's Maître d'Hotel at Buckingham Palace from 1841 to 1842, chef de cuisine to the Prince and Princess of Wales at Marlborough House from 1863 to 1865, and was also for a time manager of the St James Hotel, Piccadilly, as well as a noted author of several books on cookery?

14. A bit on the side

With which monarchs, not necessarily all of them British, would you associate the following mistresses:

1. Mathilde Kschessinska
2. Arabella Churchill
3. Elizabeth Shore
4. Lily Langtry
5. Henrietta Howard
6. Dorothea Jordan
7. Freda Dudley Ward
8. Marie Poulsen
9. Maria Fitzherbert
10. Alice Ferrers
11. Nell Gwyn
12. Rosamund Clifford

15. Now for the novels and plays

Can you identify the royal subjects of these novels from the title and the author:

1. *The Golden Prince*, Rebecca Dean
2. *The White Queen*, Philippa Gregory
3. *Royal William*, Doris Leslie
4. *Wife to the Bastard*, Hilda Lewis
5. *The Sunne in Splendour*, Sharon Kay Penman
6. *The Wild Princess*, Mary Hart Perry
7. *The She-Wolf of France*, Maurice Druon
8. *Elizabeth, Captive Princess*, Margaret Irwin
9. *The Romanov Bride*, Robert Alexander
10. *Royal Escape*, Georgette Heyer
11. *The Favoured Queen*, Carolly Erickson
12. *Queen in Waiting*, Jean Plaidy

On a similar subject, who wrote the following plays about royalty, all accompanied by their date of publication:

13. *Edward the Second* (1594)
14. *Richard of Bordeaux* (1932)
15. *Happy and Glorious* (Queen Victoria) (1943)
16. *Crown Matrimonial* (King Edward VIII and Mrs Simpson (1972)

17. *Battle Royal* (the Prince Regent and Princess Caroline of Brunswick) (1999)
18. *The Lost Prince* (Prince John, son of King George V) (2003)

16. Go on, quote me

Who said the following, or is alleged to have said:

1. 'I may be uninspiring, but I'm damned if I'm alien'
2. 'Mad, is he? Then I hope he will bite some of my other generals'
3. 'I'm glad we've been bombed. It makes me feel I can look the East End in the face'
4. 'I go from a corruptible to an incorruptible crown, where no disturbance can be, no disturbance in the world'
5. 'I declare before you all that my whole life, whether it be long or short, shall be devoted to your service and the service of our great Imperial family to which we all belong'
6. 'I know I have the body of a weak, feeble woman, but I have the heart and stomach of a King, and of a King of England too'
7. 'I cannot be indifferent to the assassination of a member of my profession; we should be obliged to shut up business if we, the Kings, were to consider the assassination of Kings as of no consequence at all'
8. 'They say that Kings are made in the image of God. If that is what He looks like, I feel sorry for God'
9. 'If it has got four legs and it is not a chair, if it has got two wings and flies but is not an

aeroplane and if it swims and it is not a submarine, the Cantonese will eat it'

10. 'You are a member of the British royal family. We are never tired, and we all love hospitals'

11. 'I regard every Social Democrat as an enemy of the Empire and Fatherland'

12. 'I never make a trip to the United States without visiting a supermarket. To me they are more fascinating than any fashion salon'

17. Dates, dates and more dates

Firstly, can you identify the reigning sovereigns (England until 1603, Great Britain thereafter) with these regnal dates?

1. 828-39
2. 871-99
3. 924-40
4. 1040-42
5. 1100-35
6. 1272-1307
7. 1377-99
8. 1422-61, 1470-71
9. 1685-88
10. 1830-37
11. 1901-10
12. 1936-52

Secondly, if you found the above questions a pushover, these might tax you rather more. From the dates and country, can you identify these European monarchs?

13. 1816-26 (Portugal)
14. 1796-1801 (Russia)
15. 1940-47 (Roumania)
16. 1951-93 (Belgium)
17. 1322-28 (France)
18. 1824-30 (France)

19. 1797-1840 (Prussia)
20. 1864-86 (Bavaria)
21. 1874-85 (Spain)
22. 1835-48 (Austria)
23. 1588-1648 (Denmark)
24. 1872-1907 (Sweden)

18. Yes, Prime Minister

Under which English or British Kings and Queens did these following Prime Ministers or major statesmen serve? In a couple of cases, the same answer is applicable to two questions:

1. Richard Neville, Earl of Warwick
2. Sir Thomas More
3. Frederick North, Lord North
4. Anthony Eden
5. John Dudley, 1st Duke of Northumberland
6. Andrew Bonar Law
7. George Hamilton-Gordon, 4th Earl of Aberdeen
8. Arthur Balfour
9. Sir Francis Walsingham
10. Arthur Wellesley, 1st Duke of Wellington
11. Benjamin Disraeli, 1st Earl of Beaconsfield
12. Ramsay MacDonald

19. Dogs and other pets

1. During whose reign were Maltese terriers first brought into Britain?
2. Eos, a puppy which was given to Prince Albert in 1833 and which came to England with him when he married Queen Victoria, was what breed?
3. What was the name of the first corgi given to Princess Elizabeth in 1944, now Queen Elizabeth II?
4. William and Greensleeves were the favourite horses of which royal siblings when they were children?
5. Which King of Italy gave Queen Victoria a Shetland pony named Alma?
6. What was Caesar, which belonged to King Edward VII, and which walked in his funeral procession?
7. Which dog was found beneath the skirts of Mary Queen of Scots after she was beheaded?
8. What was the name of the rabbit which belonged to Charles, Prince of Wales during his childhood?
9. What was Charlotte, who in pre-Health and Safety and various other food hygiene regulations, etc., was allowed by her owner King George V to help herself to anything on the breakfast table?
10. When Queen Victoria returned to Buckingham Palace after her coronation in

1838, she immediately went upstairs to give Dash his bath. What was he?

11. Which wild animal did King Charles II tame and allow to jump on his bed, thus often frightening the unsuspecting Queen Catherine?

12. When Prince Waldemar of Prussia, youngest son of the Crown Prince and Princess was staying in England with his grandmother Queen Victoria, he let Bob loose one evening and made her scream until the household came running. What was Bob?

20. A royal musical free-for-all

Some of these, I grant you, may be a little tenuous, but here goes:

1. Who had a hit in 1962 with *Your Royal Majesty*?
2. What was the name of the Sex Pistols No. 2 hit of June 1977, timed to coincide with the Queen's Silver Jubilee and banned by most shops and radio stations?
3. Which was the only hit by the group Queen to mention the word Queen in the title?
4. Which regal location in Edinburgh did Gerry Rafferty sing about in his minor hit from 1980?
5. Which royally-titled Edwardian music hall song was revived in 1965 and became an American No. 1 hit for Herman's Hermits?
6. Whose song *Thank U Very Much* originally included the line 'Thank you very much for our gracious Queen' until recommended to change the last word for fear of falling foul of BBC radio?   SCAFFOLD
7. Who had a minor hit in 1969 with *King of the Rumbling Spires*?
8. Which hit by ABBA had a royal word in the title?
9. Who had a hit in 1969 with *Victoria*, which included the refrain 'Victoria was our Queen'?

10. Who recorded an album track, *The Duke of Edinburgh's lettuce*, in 1970?

11. Who had a hit in 1978 with a song of which the refrain was 'Ra-ra-Rasputin, lover of the Russian Queen?'

12. Which hit by Supergrass was also the name of a medieval monarch, although he was not mentioned in the lyrics?

21. Abdications

In the following countries and years, the reigning monarch or sovereign prince chose to, or was asked to, renounce the throne, but which one:

1. Serbia, 1889 ?
2. Poland, 1795 ?
3. Bulgaria, 1886   FERDINAND   [ALEXANDER]
4. Netherlands, 1948   JULIANA   [WILHELMINA]
5. England, 1688   JAMES II
6. Russia, 1917   NICHOLAS II
7. Spain, 2014   F~~RANCO~~   JUAN CARLOS
8. Austria-Hungary, 1918   CHARLES
9. Sardinia, 1739 ?
10. Belgium, 2013   ALBERT II
11. Italy, 1946 ?
12. Roumania, 1947   MICHAEL ✓

22. Lucky Dip 3

1. When the house of Saxe-Coburg Gotha changed the name to the house of Windsor in 1917, which play by Shakespeare is the German Emperor William II alleged to have joked that he looked forward to seeing in performance? *The Merry Wives of Windsor*
2. Who founded the Christian Sisterhood of Martha and Mary? *Ella (Hess Darmstadt)*
3. Which monarch was known as 'The Wisest Fool in Christendom'? *James I*
4. Which future British King threatened to stand as an independent Member of Parliament for Totnes, in Devon, apparently as a protest against the delay in his father's conferring a dukedom on him? *W IV*
5. In 1961 who became the first member of the British royal family to be interviewed on TV?
6. In which European country is the reigning dynasty the house of Bernadotte?
7. The large equestrian portrait of King Charles I, bought by the National Gallery, London, in 1885, was painted by which artist?
8. Which royal couple, a monarch and his consort, narrowly escaped assassination on their wedding day, while returning to the royal palace after the ceremony, on 31 May 1906? *Alfonso XIII & Queen Ena of Spain*
9. In which year did Queen Elizabeth II first send an e-mail?

10. In which town in England was Alfred the Great born? WINCHESTER

11. Who was the only one of King Henry VIII's wives to be given a state funeral? JANE SEYMOUR

12. Who is the only sovereign to have been born and died at Buckingham Palace?

13. Which Queen of England, a Queen consort, never once set foot inside the British Isles?

14. Who was the last reigning sovereign of Britain to have been born outside the British Isles? GEORGE ii

15. Who was born at 17 Bruton Street, Mayfair, on 21 April 1926? EII

16. Prior to the death of Queen Victoria, King George III's reign of 59 years was the longest since the Norman Conquest; at 56 years, whose was the second longest?

17. Queen Mary, wife of King George V, had three brothers; one was Adolphus, Marquis of Cambridge; one was Frank, Duke of Teck; who was the other?

18. Who held the Royal Warrant as Dressmaker to Queen Elizabeth from 1940, and Royal Warrant as Dressmaker to Queen Elizabeth II in 1957, and also designed clothes for her until shortly before his death in 1979? NORMAN HARTNELL

19. Which British Queen Consort died in November 1925? QUEEN ALEXANDRA

20. Who was the only King of the Norman dynasty who never married? W ii

21. With whose death in 1807 did the royal house of Stuart become extinct in the male line?

22. At which castle was Henry Tudor, later King Henry VII, born?

23. Why was Henrietta Maria, Consort of King Charles I, never crowned Queen of England?

24. Which artist painted the full-length portraits of allied heads of state during the early nineteenth century which hang in the Waterloo Chamber, Windsor Castle?

25. At which royal residence did King George V and King George VI both die?

23. Armed forces

Members of British royalty have long had a tradition of close involvement with the services; can you answer these?

1. As heir to the throne, Queen Elizabeth II became the first female member of the royal family to be a full-time active member of the Services when she joined which unit in 1945?
2. Which future King served in New York during the American War of Independence, and almost became the target of a kidnap plot approved by George Washington?
3. During which conflict did Andrew, Duke of York, serve with the Navy as a second pilot in Sea King Helicopters on anti-submarine and transport duties?
4. Which prince earned his pilot's licence in 1929 and became the first member of the royal family to cross the Atlantic by air?
5. After leaving Gordonstoun in 1939 Prince Philip, later Duke of Edinburgh, joined the Navy, and graduated the following year as the top cadet in his course from which establishment?
6. Which regiment did the Prince of Wales, later King Edward VIII, join in June 1914 just before the outbreak of war?
7. Where in England did Alfred, Duke of Edinburgh, serve as Commander-in-Chief from 1890 to 1893?

8. Who served as Commander-in-Chief of the Mediterranean Fleet from 1952 to 1954, First Sea Lord from 1955 to 1959, and Chief of the Defence Staff from 1959 to 1965?

9. Who was Commander-in-Chief of the Army from 1856 to 1895?

10. Where did Charles, Prince of Wales, begin his career in the services in 1971?

11. Who was Commander-in-Chief in Ireland from 1900 to 1904, and Inspector-General of the Forces from 1904 to 1907?

12. Which unit did Henry, Duke of Gloucester serve as Chief Liaison Officer after the outbreak of the Second World War?

24. Who and who, or whom, or what

A few more royal quotations – who said the following to whom?

1. *'Non, j'aurai des maitresses'* ('No, I shall have mistresses')
2. 'You have no right to drag your relatives with you down a precipice'
3. 'I am sure no man in England will take away my life to make you King'
4. 'God damn it, why don't you drink wine? I never allow anyone to drink water at my table'
5. 'We invented the postage stamp—all it had on it was the sovereign's head and postage and its value. That's all we want'
6. 'You've been pretty unlucky with the weather, Mr Piper'

Who made or is alleged to have made the following remarks, and about whom or what?

7. 'He speaks to me as if I were a public meeting'
8. 'He was the most extraordinary compound of talent, wit, buffoonery, obstinacy, and good feelings, in short, a medley of the most opposite qualities, with a great

preponderance of good – that I ever saw in any character in my life'

9. 'It is not by his will that he will unleash a war, but by his weakness'

10. 'If the Princess can leave the Englishwoman at home and become a Prussian, then she may become a blessing to the country'

11. 'Mindful of the Church's teaching that Christian marriage is indissoluble, and conscious of my duty to the Commonwealth, I have resolved to put these considerations before any others'

12. 'A higher power has restored the old order which I unfortunately was unable to uphold'

25. The big picture

Can you identify the following feature films from the brief description, names of the main stars and the year in which they were released?

1. The relationship between Queen Victoria and her Highland ghillie; Judi Dench, Billy Connolly, 1997   *MRS BROWN*
2. The mental illness of the longest-lived Hanoverian monarch; Nigel Hawthorne, Helen Mirren, 1994   *THE MADNESS OF KING GEORGE*
3. The tragic life and death of the last Queen of Scotland; Vanessa Redgrave, Glenda Jackson, 1971
4. The early years of the reign and marriage of the longest reigning British Queen; Emily Blunt, Rupert Friend, 2009   *YOUNG VICTORIA*
5. Two sisters are rivals for the affection of King Henry VIII; Natalie Portman, Scarlett Johansson, Eric Bana, 2008   *THE OTHER BOLEYN GIRL*
6. The royal family come to terms with the implication of Princess Diana's death; Helen Mirren, Michael Sheen, 2006
7. A Tudor Queen's love-hate relationship with one of her leading favourites at court; Bette Davis, Errol Flynn, 1939
8. The last Tsar of Russia and his family are forced to renounce the throne and end their days in captivity; Michael Jayston, Janet Suzman, 1971   *NICHOLAS AND ALEXANDRA*

9. Aided by his therapist, a King tries to overcome his stammer; Colin Firth, Geoffrey Rush, Helena Bonham-Carter, 2010 *The King's Speech*

10. King Henry VIII is determined to end his first marriage and take a second wife; Richard Burton, Genevieve Bujold, Irene Papas, 1969 *Anne of a Thousand Days*

11. A Scandinavian Queen falls in love with her Spanish envoy, and must choose between him and her throne; Greta Garbo, John Gilbert, 1933 *A Christina*

12. King Henry II's three sons want to inherit his throne, and with their mother conspire against him; Peter O'Toole, Katherine Hepburn, 1968 *The Lion in Winter*

26. Another quotation round

Who said, or is supposed to have said, the following:

1. 'What does it matter if I am killed? I have four brothers'
2. 'There were three of us in this marriage, so it was a bit crowded'
3. 'Don't fancy that, for there are six more of us, and they don't want us'
4. 'My children are not royal; they just happen to have the Queen for their aunt'
5. 'I think people in general consider us a mere passing shadow, soon to be replaced in reality by the shape of William'
6. 'My father was frightened of his mother; I was frightened of my father, and I am damned well going to see to it that my children are frightened of me'
7. 'I trust in God that my life may be spared for nine months longer, after which period, in the event of my death, no Regency would take place. I should then have the satisfaction of leaving the Royal authority to the personal exercise of that young lady [Princess Victoria, later Queen], the heiress presumptive to the Crown, and not in the hands of a person now near me [Victoria's mother, Duchess of Kent], who is surrounded by evil advisers and who is

herself incompetent to act with propriety in the station in which she would be placed'

8. 'You are a pest, by the very nature of that camera in your hand'

9. 'I shall be an autocrat, that's my trade; and the good Lord will forgive me, that's His'

10. 'The children could not possibly go without me, I wouldn't leave without the King, and the King will never leave'

11. 'I have committed every vice but one and I do not intend to die before I have killed a man'

12. 'The whole world is in revolt. Soon there will be only five Kings left – the King of England, the King of Spades, the King of Clubs, the King of Hearts, and the King of Diamonds'

27. Politicians

The answers to these questions are all senior British politicians, mostly Prime Ministers:

1. Which Postmaster-General suggested in 1965 to Queen Elizabeth II that future British postage stamps could be issued without the sovereign's head?
2. Which backbench Member of Parliament published the republican tract *My Queen and I* in 1975?
3. Who was Prime Minister at the time of the Edward VIII abdication crisis?
4. Which Prime Minister did King William IV ask for his resignation in November 1834, but had to recall in April 1835?
5. Which Prime Minister said he would advise his successor to do his homework before the weekly meeting with Queen Elizabeth II, or he would feel like an unprepared schoolboy?
6. Which leader of the Long Parliament during the reign of King Charles I negotiated the Solemn League and Covenant, thus gaining support for Parliament from the Scottish Presbyterians?
7. Which French-born nobleman led the rebellion against King Henry III and called two Parliaments, but was defeated and killed at the battle of Evesham by forces who remained loyal to the sovereign?

8. Which Prime Minister declared that King George V seemed to be 'hostile to the bone to all who are working to lift the workmen out of the mire?'

9. Which minister did Clement Attlee plan to appoint Foreign Secretary in 1945, but was instead appointed Chancellor of the Exchequer, after King George VI privately expressed his reservations?

10. Which Prime Minister was summoned urgently from an emergency cabinet meeting when Queen Elizabeth II needed to discuss the crisis which followed the American invasion of Grenada?

11. Which Prime Minister said that everybody loves flattery, but when it comes to royalty you must lay it on with a trowel?

12. Which Labour minister was a great favourite of King George V, and once told him a joke at which the sovereign laughed so much that he split a post-operative wound from lung abscess surgery?

28. A question of sport

Royalty on the racecourse, on the tennis court, on the water, and at the Olympics as well:

1. King Edward VII was the first reigning British monarch to win the Derby in 1909, but what was the name of his winning horse?
2. Who was the aide-de-camp of Lord Spencer, whom he selected to pilot Elizabeth, Empress of Austria, when she visited England and rode with the hunt at Althorp in the 1870s?
3. Which crime writer was jockey to Queen Elizabeth the Queen Mother from 1953 to 1957?
4. Which European monarch had several yachts named *Hohenzollern* and *Meteor*?
5. Which heir to the throne became captain of Walton Heath Golf Club in 1935?
6. Golf and which other sport was banned by the Scots Parliament of King James II in 1457 'to preserve the skills of archery'?
7. Which grandson of Queen Victoria was the only member of the royal family to play first class cricket?
8. Which cricket-loving heir to the throne was said, probably wrongly, to have died in 1751 after being hit by a cricket ball?
9. Which royal tennis enthusiast competed in 1926 in the men's doubles at Wimbledon?

10. Which horse belonging to Queen Elizabeth II won the Epsom Oaks and the St Leger Stakes in her Silver Jubilee year of 1977?

11. Which future King of Greece won a gold medal in the Dragon class sailing event at the Rome Olympics in 1960?

12. In the 1912 summer Olympics in Stockholm, Grand Duke Dmitri Paulovitch of Russia competed in the team jumping equestrian event against which nephew of the German Empress?

29. Bagehot

Walter Bagehot published *The English Constitution* in 1867. Can you fill in the blank spaces from the following extracts? Note – ten of these are British monarchs, one is European, and for a generous clue, one is the mother of a British monarch who never reigned herself but would have done so if only she had lived for another few weeks.

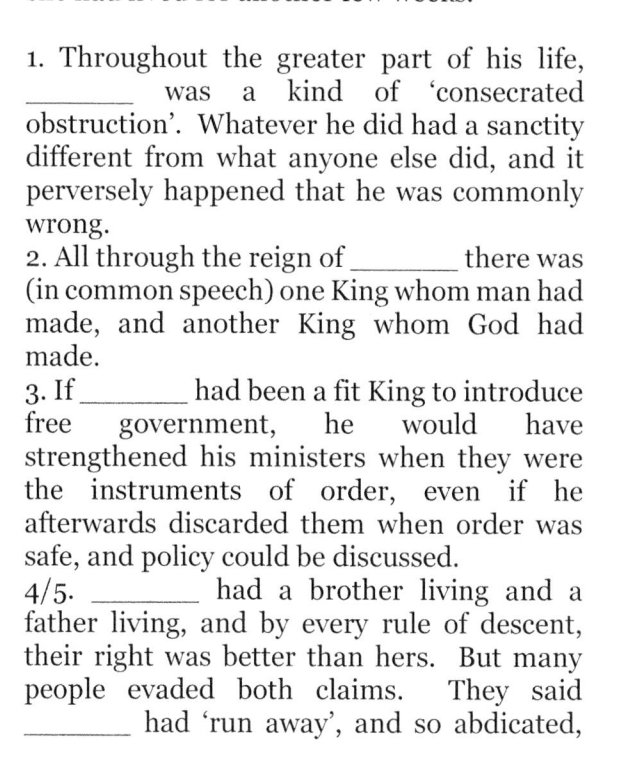

1. Throughout the greater part of his life, _____ was a kind of 'consecrated obstruction'. Whatever he did had a sanctity different from what anyone else did, and it perversely happened that he was commonly wrong.
2. All through the reign of _____ there was (in common speech) one King whom man had made, and another King whom God had made.
3. If _____ had been a fit King to introduce free government, he would have strengthened his ministers when they were the instruments of order, even if he afterwards discarded them when order was safe, and policy could be discussed.
4/5. _____ had a brother living and a father living, and by every rule of descent, their right was better than hers. But many people evaded both claims. They said _____ had 'run away', and so abdicated,

though he only ran away because he was in duress and was frightened, and though he claimed the allegiance of his subjects day by day.

6/7. According to the Act of Settlement passed by the Whigs, the crown was settled on the descendants of the _____, a younger daughter of a daughter of _____.

8/9/10/11. Neither _____, nor _____, nor _____, were patterns of family merit; _____ was a model of family _____.

12. We have come to regard the crown as the head of our *morality*. The virtues of _____ and the virtues of George III have sunk deep into the popular heart.

30. Shakespeare

Can you identify the characters, some but not all of them crowned heads, from the history plays of William Shakespeare who spoke the following lines – and maybe award yourself a bonus point or two if you succeed in getting the relevant plays as well?

1. 'Then God forgive the sins of all those souls,
   That to their everlasting residence,
   Before the dew of evening fall, shall fleet
   In dreadful trial of our kingdom's king!'
2. 'Your strong possession, much more than your right,
   Or else it must go wrong with you, and me:
   So much my conscience whispers in your ear,
   Which none but heaven, and you, and I, shall hear.'
3. 'For God's sake, let us sit upon the ground
   And tell sad stories of the death of kings;
   How some have been deposed; some slain in war,
   Some haunted by the ghosts they have deposed.'
4. 'This royal throne of kings, this sceptr'd isle,
   This earth of majesty, this seat of Mars,
   This other Eden, demi-paradise,
   This fortress built by Nature for herself

    Against infection and the hand of war.'
5. 'O, that it could be proved
    That some night-tripping fairy had exchanged
    In cradle clothes our children where they lay,
    And called mine Percy, his Plantagenet!'
6. 'Once more unto the breach, dear friends, once more,
    Or close the wall up with our English dead!
    In peace there's nothing so becomes a man
    As modest stillness and humility.'
7. 'Is this the fashion in the court of England?
    Is this the government of Britain's isle,
    And this the royalty of Albion's king?'
8. 'Break thou in pieces, and consume to ashes,
    Thou foul accursed minister of hell.'
9. 'What stronger breast-plate than a heart untainted!
    Thrice is he arm'd, that hath his quarrel just;
    And he but naked, though lock'd up in steel,
    Whose conscience with injustice is corrupted.'
10. 'Now is the winter of our discontent
    Made glorious summer by this sun of York;
    And all the clouds that lour'd upon our house
    In the deep bosom of the ocean buried.'
11. 'Oh, I have passed a miserable night,
    So full of fearful dreams, of ugly sights,
    That, as I am a Christian faithful man,
    I would not spend another such a night.'
12. 'Pray you, arise,
    My good and gracious Lord of Canterbury.

Come, you and I must walk a turn together;
I have news to tell you: come, come, give me your hand.'

31. 1066 And All That

In 1930 W.C. Sellar and R.J. Yeatman published *1066 And All That: A Memorable History of England*, a splendid work of humour which has delighted several generations and, though it might seem dated to younger readers today, has been reprinted several times. As its authors would have said, it was a Good Thing. Can you identify the monarchs which are being referred to in the following brief extracts, all in chronological order?

1. 'This monarch was always very angry and red in the face and was therefore unpopular, so that his death was a Good Thing.'
2. '____ was famous for his handwriting and was therefore generally called ____ Beaugeste. He was extremely fond of his son William, who was, however, drowned in the White City.'
3. '____ was a hairy King with a Lion's Heart; he went roaring about the Desert making ferocious attacks on the Saladins and the Paladins, and was thus a very romantic King.'
4. '____ was a confused kind of King and is only memorable for having seized all the money in the Mint, imprisoned himself in the Tower of London and, finally, flung himself into the Bosom of the Pope.'

5. '___ had a very romantic reign which he began by confining his mother in a stronghold for the rest of her life, and inventing a law called the Gallic Law according to which he was King of France, and could therefore make war on it whenever he felt inclined.'

6. '___ was a miser and very good at statecraft; he invented some extremely clever policies such as the one called Morton's Fork.'

7. 'JI slobbered at the mouth and had favourites; he was thus a Bad King. He had, however, a very logical and tidy mind, and one of the first things he did was to have Sir Walter Raleigh executed for being left over from the previous reign.'

8. 'CII was always very merry and was therefore not so much a King as a Monarch. During the civil war he had rendered valuable assistance to his father's side by hiding in all the oak trees he could find.'

9. 'Although a Good Man, ___ was a Bad King and behaved in such an irritating and arbitrary way that by the end of his reign the people had all gone mad.'

10. 'GIII was a Bad King. He was, however, to a great extent insane and a Good Man and his ministers were always called Pitt.'

11. 'WIV was known as the Sailor King on account of his readiness to create any number of piers at moments of political crisis.'

12. 'EVII was really a very active man and had many romantic occupations; for instance, he went betting and visited Paris and was sometimes late for dinner; in addition he was merry with actresses and kind to gypsies.'

32. Farjeon's Kings and Queens

Another classic from the same era, Eleanor and Herbert Farjeon's *Kings and Queens*, published in 1932 and again frequently reissued since, was a book of rhymes for children but much cherished by adults as well. Once again, can you identify the subjects from the following lines, all in chronological order?

1. 'By the Saxons he conquered was hated and cursed,
   And they planned and they plotted far into the night.'
2. 'Who, sure of aim,
   And never afraid,
   Was always game
   For a good Crusade.'
3. 'Not a scruple, not a straw,
   Cared this monarch for the law;
   Promises he daily broke;
   None could trust a word he spoke.'
4. 'He had the longest legs of all,
   But when from one who wished him harm
   A poisoned dagger pierced his arm,
   ___ was as weak as other men.'
5. '___ is commonly reckoned
   One of the feeblest of all our kings.
   Favours he lavished on

Pretty Piers Gaveston,
   Giving him duchies and riches and rings.'
6. '___ was a wild boy,
   Fond of fun and fooling;
   When he was the Prince of Wales
   He made a hash of schooling.'
7. 'He'd a voice like silk,
   And manners like milk,
   And a smile that was most disarming.'
8. 'Alas for this nice little, poor little lad!
   His reign was the shortest that any king had.'
9. '"Alas!" quoth she to those who tried
   To soothe her grief and heal her pride,
   "You'll find when I this life depart
   Calais engraved upon my heart!"'
10. 'She's vain as a peacock that opens its tail,
    She's proud as an eagle that weathers the gale,
    She's crafty and jealous, suspicious and mean,
    But England *is* England now ___ is the Queen.'
11. 'If she was plain,
    She had a pretty fan,
    If she was dull,
    She wore a pretty gown.'
12. '___, he often goes
    To Brighton for a spree,
    Where all the bucks and all the beaux
    Parade beside the sea.'

33. Lucky Dip 4

1. Which sculptor was responsible for the statue of Queen Victoria which stands in Windsor High Street, just below the castle?
2. Who was born at Glamis Castle on 21 August 1930?
3. Who was the last King of the Two Sicilies, 1859-61, before his territory and the kingdom of Sardinia were merged into the kingdom of Italy?
4. Who designed the head of Queen Elizabeth II which was used on British coins from 1968 to 1984, and on British definitive stamps from 1967 onwards?
5. Which Prince of Liechtenstein enjoyed the longest reign in European royal history since the beginning of the nineteenth century?
6. Who was born at Park House, Sandringham, on 1 July 1961?
7. Lytton Strachey, Sidney Lee, Elizabeth Longford, Alison Plowden, Giles St Aubyn, Christopher Hibbert, Stanley Weintraub and A.N. Wilson have all published biographies of whom?
8. Which Spanish dictator nominated King Juan Carlos I as his successor after his death?
9. If Mrs Freeman was Sarah, Duchess of Marlborough, who was Mrs Morley?
10. Which Australian city was named after a nineteenth-century British Queen Consort?

11. Dom Pedro II, who reigned from 1831 to 1889, was the last ruler of which American empire?

12. Prince Philip, Duke of Edinburgh, is said to have once likened a sculpture by whom to a 'monkey's gallstone'?

13. Which European monarch abdicated in favour of his twelve-year-old son in 1889 and died in Vienna in February 1901?

14. As he went into exile in 1689, what did the former King James II drop into the Thames?

15. In 2006 King Bhumibol Adulyadej celebrated sixty years on the throne of which Asian country?

16. Which German-Swiss artist came to England in around 1526 and was employed as King's Painter to King Henry VIII from around 1535 onwards?

17. Who wrote articles on farming under the name of Ralph Robinson?

18. The Amalienborg is the winter home of which European royal family?

19. In the James Bond-themed sketch shown during the opening ceremony of the London Olympics in 2012, which Bond actor appeared alongside Queen Elizabeth II?

20. Edward of Middleham, Prince of Wales, who died at the age of ten, was the only legitimate child of which English King?

21. Where in England did the former Emperor Napoleon, Empress Eugenie and their son the Prince Imperial settle during their exile until the Emperor's death in 1873?

22. Which sister of King Charles II died of smallpox at Whitehall Palace while on a visit to England?

23. Which future King of England was created Duke of York and Lieutenant of Ireland in 1494, at the age of three?

24. By what name is Edward of Woodstock, an heir to the throne who predeceased his father the King, better known?

25. Who was the second wife of King John of England?

34. The Normans

1. Which area north-east of Southampton was requisitioned by King William I as an exclusive hunting ground for the sovereign and his party, and remains a national park to this day?
2. Who was elected King of England in October 1066 after the death of King Harold II at the battle of Hastings, in preference to William of Normandy, his election being set aside about two months later?
3. Who was the second wife and consort of King Henry I?
4. By what name is William I's inventory of the country, completed around 1086, known to posterity?
5. Who was King William I's eldest son and heir to his dukedom of Normandy?
6. At which battle in February 1141 was King Stephen captured and subsequently imprisoned by Empress Matilda?
7. To which town did King Henry I go and demand the keys of the treasury on the death of King William II, in order to establish a claim to the throne while their eldest brother Robert was still away on the First Crusade?
8. Which castle was built by order of King William II to keep the northern border secure against the threat of invasion from Scotland, with construction beginning around 1093?

9. Which Archbishop of Canterbury was exiled by William II from 1097 but returned during the reign of King Henry I?

10. Which nephew of King Henry I did he support in his disputes against King Louis VI of France?

11. Where in England was King Henry I buried?

12. By the terms of which treaty in 1153 did King Stephen agree that on his death the throne would go to Matilda's son Henry?

35. The Plantagenets

For the purposes of this book, the Plantagenets are regarded as the dynasty which reigned from 1154 to 1399, with the Lancastrians and Yorkists treated separately in the two rounds which follow.

1. Who was the Archbishop of Canterbury murdered in his cathedral in 1170 by four knights, misinterpreting an expression of impatience by King Henry II as a royal command to execute him?
2. Which foreign sovereign married King Henry II's daughter Eleanor in 1177?
3. Also in 1177, the future King John was given the lordship of which country?
4. At which battle in south-west France was King Henry II defeated by his eldest surviving son Richard in July 1189, two days before his death?
5. Where was King Richard II born?
6. Where were Prince Edward, later King Edward I, and Eleanor married in 1154?
7. Who was the lover of Queen Isabella, husband of King Edward II, who helped to depose the latter in 1327?
8. At which naval battle in 1340 at the start of the Hundred Years War was King Edward III present?

9. Which is the most senior and the oldest British Order of Chivalry, founded by Edward III in 1348?

10. Which title was bestowed on Henry Bolingbroke by King Richard II in 1397?

11. Where was King Richard II imprisoned after his abdication in 1399 and thought to have been starved to death?

12. The legitimate male issue of the Plantagenet line became extinct in 1499 with whose execution?

36. The Lancastrians

1. From which son of King Edward III were Kings Henry IV, V and VI descended?
2. Who was the Archbishop of York and Bishop of Lichfield, executed in 1406 after his participation in the northern rising against King Henry IV?
3. Which town in northern France surrendered to King Henry V in January 1419?
4. By which treaty of May 1420 was King Henry V recognised as heir to the French throne and regent of France?
5. Who was the father of Margaret of Anjou, who became the consort of King Henry VI in 1445?
6. King Henry IV's daughter Philippa married which King of Denmark, Norway and Sweden in 1406?
7. Which charity school was founded by King Henry VI in or about 1440 to provide free education for around 70 poor boys to go on later to King's College, Cambridge?
8. Henry Percy ('Hotspur'), who led a rebellion against King Henry IV, was defeated and killed at which battle in 1403?
9. In which year was King Henry VI declared of age, and subsequently assumed the reins of government?
10. Who led a rebellion in 1450 in Kent against the government of King Henry VI?

11. Which son of King Henry IV was killed at the battle of Baugé in 1421?
12. At which battle was Prince Edward, only son of King Henry VI, slain?

37. The Yorkists

1. After which battle in July 1460 was King Henry VI captured in his tent and escorted first to Delapre Abbey, then London?
2. To which position was Richard, Duke of York, appointed in 1436 in succession to John of Lancaster, Duke of Bedford, who had died the previous year?
3. Richard, Duke of York, father of the future King Edward IV and Richard III, was killed at the battle of Wakefield in December 1460, as was which of his sons?
4. At which battle did Edward, Earl of March and shortly to become King Edward IV, defeat a Lancastrian force in February 1461?
5. Who led the victorious Yorkist army at the battle of Hexham in May 1464?
6. Elizabeth Woodville wad the widow of which Lancastrian knight, who was killed at the second battle of St Albans in 1461?
7. When King Edward IV declared wear on France in 1475, which of his French allies failed to provide him with any military aid and thus forced him to negotiate for peace with the French?
8. Which title was held by King Edward IV before he became King in March 1461?
9. At which treaty did King Edward IV make his peace with King Louis XI of France in 1475?

10. The Duke of Gloucester led an invasion of Scotland in 1482 in which Alexander, Duke of Albany, was attempting to seize the Scottish throne from which King, who was his brother?

11. After fleeing to Holland in 1470, where in France did King Edward IV take refuge before returning to England to reclaim his crown the following year?

12. Which nobleman was the Duke of Gloucester's most ardent supporter when he claimed the throne in 1483, but then turned traitor, led an unsuccessful rebellion in October 1483, was captured and executed early the following month?

38. King Henry VII

1. Who was the mother of Henry?
2. Where, on Christmas Day 1483, did Henry pledge to marry Elizabeth of York?
3. Who was designated heir by King Richard III and reconciled at first with King Henry VII, but then implicated in the Yorkist rebellion and killed at the battle of Stoke in 1487?
4. Which Pope did King Henry VII persuade to issue a Papal Bull of Excommunication against all pretenders to his throne?
5. When King Henry VII concluded the Treaty of Perpetual Peace with Scotland in 1502, which member of his family became betrothed to King James IV?
6. After Perkin Warbeck landed in Cornwall in 1497 intending to claim the throne and advanced east, where was he captured and was forced to surrender?
7. Following the death of Queen Elizabeth in 1503, in which foreign Queen did King Henry VII show interest as a potential second wife?
8. Which treaty with Spain in 1489 provided for the establishment of a common policy for both countries regarding France, the reduction of tariffs between them, and the arrangement of a marriage contract between King Henry VII's eldest son Prince Arthur and Catherine of Aragon?

9. The first husband of King Henry VII's younger daughter Mary was King Louis XIII of France; who was the second?

10. As Henry's father Edmund Tudor died before he was born, who was the uncle who became the guardian of his mother and himself?

11. Who was King Henry VII's Archbishop of Canterbury and Lord Chancellor who was charged with restoring the royal estate by means of an economic policy of new taxation and forced loans to be paid by the nobility?

12. What was the English court of law set up at the Palace of Westminster under King Henry VII, consisting of Privy Councillors and common law judges, to ensure the fair enforcement of laws against prominent people?

39. King Henry VIII

1. Where was the future Henry VIII born?
2. In 1503 Henry was created Prince of Wales. Which earldom was conferred on him at the same time?
3. Which of Henry's mistresses was the mother of his son Henry FitzRoy, Duke of Richmond?
4. The Field of the Cloth of Gold near Calais was the site of a meeting in France in June 1520 between Henry and which French King?
5. Which title did Pope Leo X confer on Henry in October 1521, the initials of which still appear alongside the Queen's head on today's coinage?
6. What was the name of Henry's elder brother, Prince of Wales, who was originally married to Catherine of Aragon but died of the sweating sickness at the age of fifteen in April 1502?
7. When Henry and his army invaded France in 1513, at which battle was he victorious?
8. Which of Henry's chief ministers was charged with and found guilty of treason, selling export licences, granting passports, and drawing up commissions without permission, attainted and executed in July 1540?
9. On which of his Queens did Henry confer the title Marquess of Pembroke?

10. Which Act, passed in 1534, declared that the King was the only Supreme Head on Earth of the Church of England?

11. In 1503 Henry's sister Margaret married which Scottish King, who was killed in battle ten years later?

12. Which of Henry's warships sank in the Solent in action against the French fleet in July 1545 with the loss of most of its crew?

40. King Edward VI and Queen Mary I

1. Who was the mother of King Edward VI? *Jane Seymour*
2. Who was nominated as his heir by King Edward VI, and reigned for nine days, but was executed in 1554? *Lady Jane Grey*
3. Which battle was fought between the English and Scottish in September 1547 as part of the English campaign to secure a marriage between King Edward VI and Mary, Queen of Scots?
4. Where in Hertfordshire did Edward and Mary live for several years before each ascended the throne in turn?
5. Who was the last Roman Catholic Archbishop of Canterbury, and who died a few hours after Queen Mary herself?
6. Which Professor of Greek at Cambridge University was appointed King Edward VI's regular tutor?
7. Where were Queen Mary and King Philip II of Spain married in July 1554?
8. Which Archbishop of Canterbury was tried for treason and heresy after the accession of Queen Mary and burnt at the stake in March 1556?
9. Which was England's last possession in France, lost in January 1558 after England went to France as an ally of Spain?

10. Who led the rebellion in Kent in January 1554 in protest at the forthcoming marriage of Queen Mary and King Philip II?

11. Who was the Protestant Bishop of Exeter and translator of the Bible whom Queen Mary allowed to leave England and settle in Denmark?

12. Who wrote *A First Blast Of The Trumpet Against The Monstrous Regiment Of Women,* a pamphlet attacking the rule of Queen Mary?

41. Queen Elizabeth I

1. Who was the mother of the future Queen Elizabeth?
2. Where was Elizabeth in November 1558 when she was brought the news of the death of her sister Queen Mary and that she had therefore succeeded to the throne?
3. Who was appointed her governess when she was aged four, and remained a friend until her death in 1565?
4. Who was Lord High Steward at the Queen's Coronation in January 1559?
5. At her coronation Queen Elizabeth was crowned and anointed by Owen Oglethorpe, the Catholic bishop of which diocese?
6. Who founded a colony in North America and named it Virginia in Queen Elizabeth's honour?
7. Who was Queen Elizabeth's second cousin who was executed in 1572 after being implicated in the Ridolfi plot?
8. Who was appointed Queen Elizabeth's Master of the Horse in 1559, and nominated as Protector of the Realm in case of any possible emergencies after her recovery from smallpox in 1562?
9. What was the name of Edmund Spenser's epic poem celebrating the Tudor dynasty and in particular the Queen?

10. Who was appointed Queen Elizabeth's Captain of the Yeomen of the Guard in 1572 and her Lord Chancellor in 1587?

11. To which country did Queen Elizabeth send the Earl of Essex to put down a revolt in the spring of 1599?

12. In 1579 there was speculation about Queen Elizabeth's possible marriage to which French Roman Catholic figure?

42. The early Stuarts

1. Who was the father of King James VI and I?
2. James was crowned King of Scotland at the age of thirteen months, at which church?
3. Of which territory was King James's son-in-law Frederick, Elector Palatine from 1610 to 1623, King from 1619 to 1620?
4. Who was the favourite at court of King James during the last years of his reign, and given the nickname 'Steenie' after St Stephen, as he was said to have had 'the face of an angel'?
5. King James only returned to Scotland once after the union of the crowns and his accession, in order to implement Anglican ritual there – in which year?
6. Which Act of Parliament was passed under King James in 1606, by which any citizen could be required to take an oath of allegiance denying the Pope's authority over the King?
7. What relation was Prince Rupert of the Rhine, commander of the Royalist cavalry during the Civil War until banished from England after the siege and surrender of Oxford in 1646, to King Charles I?
8. In which city did King Charles I make his headquarters throughout much of the Civil War?
9. Who was the father of Queen Henrietta Maria, consort of King Charles I?

10. Which tax was levied by King Charles I from 1634 onwards to pay for the Royal Navy?

11. When King Charles went on trial for treason, on what grounds did he refuse to recognise the legality of the court?

12. Where was Henrietta, later Duchesse d'Orléans, the youngest child of King Charles and Queen Henrietta Maria, born?

43. King Charles II and King James II

1. Which title was conferred on the future King James II in 1644?
2. By which proclamation, issued in April 1660, did King Charles II promise to grant a general pardon for crimes committed during the English civil war and interregnum for all those who promised to recognise him as the lawful sovereign?
3. Which Act of Parliament passed in 1662 under King Charles II made use of the Anglican Book of Common Prayer compulsory?
4. Which treaty did King Charles II conclude with King Louis XIV of France in 1670, by which he agreed that he would convert to Catholicism at a later unspecified date?
5. Which Lord Chancellor was the father-in-law of the future King James II?
6. What was the name of the conspiracy in 1683 in which it was planned to assassinate King Charles II and his brother, later King James II?
7. By what collective name were King Charles II's closest advisers, Lord Clifford, Lord Arlington, the Duke of Buckingham, Lord Ashley and Lord Lauderdale, known?
8. Who led the Scottish rebellion against King James II in 1685?

9. At which battle off the east coast did James, while Lord High Admiral, win a battle during the Second Anglo-Dutch War in July 1665?

10. When James was appointed Lord High Commissioner of Scotland in 1680 to oversee royal government, where did he reside?

11. Which Scottish peer led a rebellion against King James II shortly after his accession, but was captured and executed in June 1685?

12. Charles Palmer, Lord Limerick and later Duke of Southampton, was the son of King Charles II by which of his mistresses?

44. King William III, Queen Mary II and Queen Anne

1. At which town on the south-west coast of England did William of Orange and his army land in November 1688?
2. What was the name given to the Parliament summoned by William which met in January 1689, shortly before he was acknowledged as King, to discuss the appropriate course of action following the flight of King James II at the end of the previous year?
3. Which Bishop of London was tutor to Mary and Anne while they were young, subsequently married William and Mary at St James's Palace in 1677, and also crowned them at Westminster Abbey in 1689?
4. Which treaty ended the Nine Years' War, signed in September 1697?
5. In which year did King William III grant the Royal Charter to the Bank of England?
6. Who led the Highland revolt in support of the former King James II and led his forces to victory at the battle of Killiecrankie in July 1869, although he was killed in the fighting?
7. Which treaty ended the Williamite war in Ireland between the supporters of William III and James II, signed in 1691?

8. Who did Princess, later Queen, Anne marry in July 1683?

9. Who did Queen Anne appoint Master-General of the Ordnance and Captain-General of the armies at home and abroad?

10. Who was the ringleader of the Jacobite plot to assassinate King William III in 1696, and executed the following year?

11. From which bill did Queen Anne withhold royal assent in 1708 in case the troops proved disloyal to the crown?

12. In which battle, fought in Ireland in July 1690, did King William III win a victory over the former King James II?

45. King George I

1. By which Act of Parliament of 1701 was Sophia, Electress of Hanover, designated heir to the English throne if King William III and his sister-in-law and heir Anne should die without issue, as indeed they did?
2. With which British order of chivalry was Prince George invested in August 1701, a year before he ascended the British throne?
3. In which year did George I succeed his father as Elector of Hanover?
4. Where was King George I initially buried?
5. Who was the lover of King George I's estranged wife Sophia Dorothea, who (the lover) was killed in 1694?
6. Who did George I's daughter Sophia Dorothea marry in 1796?
7. King George I spoke French as well as German, but not a word of English – true or false?
8. During the Jacobite rebellion of 1715, which Scottish nobleman led the forces in Scotland on behalf of James Stuart (the Old Pretender) in their futile rebellion against George I?
9. What was the name of the Act passed by the Whig-dominated Parliament in 1715, which extended the maximum duration of Parliament to seven years?

10. Who was appointed George I's First Lord of the Treasury and Lord President of the Council in 1718?

11. By what name is the financial crisis of 1720, which made King George I and his ministers very unpopular, generally known?

12. Which order of chivalry did George I revive in 1725, thus enabling his chief minister to use it as a reward or to gain political supporters by offering them the honour?

46. King George II

1. In which battle of the War of the Spanish Succession, fought against the French in July 1708, did the future King George II take part as a commander in the Hanoverian cavalry?
2. When the future King George II visited the court of Ansbach to meet the princess who would become his wife in June 1705, under which assumed name did he travel?
3. When Prince George and Princess Caroline left Hanover for England in 1714 on the succession of his father as King George I, who was their uncle in Hanover in whose care they left their eldest son Frederick?
4. Where in 1716 was an unsuccessful attempt made on Prince George's life?
5. Who was the Lord Chamberlain with whom George II, as Prince of Wales, had an argument at the christening of his son George William in November 1717?
6. Who commanded the royal forces at the battle of Culloden in 1746?
7. What was the name of George II's mistress, whose title was Countess of Suffolk?
8. Which royal doctor attended Queen Caroline in her last and fatal illness in 1737?
9. At which battle of the War of the Austrian Succession in June 1743 did King George II personally take command of his troops?
10 Who did George II's youngest daughter Louisa marry in 1743?

11. Of which future son-in-law did George II say to his daughter, 'Well, then, there is baboon enough for you'?

12. Who was appointed Serjeant Painter to George II in 1757?

47. King George III

1. As a baby, Prince George was baptised by the Rector of St James's and the Bishop of Oxford; what was his name?
2. Which title was conferred on Prince George after the death of his father Frederick, Prince of Wales, in 1751?
3. Who made an attempt on the King's life in August 1786 as he alighted from a carriage outside St James's Palace?
4. Which law forbidding descendants of King George II to marry without the sovereign's consent, introduced at the King's request, was passed by Parliament in 1772?
5. Which of the King's daughters died in 1810, his grief at her death being said to have been partly responsible for the subsequent decline in his mental health?
6. Which astronomer discovered the planet Uranus in 1781 and initially named it Georgius Sidus (Georgian star) in the King's honour?
7. At which town on the coast of Dorset did the King take his summer break on a regular basis between 1789 and 1805?
8. Which title did King George relinquish in 1801 after the union of Great Britain and Ireland?
9. Who died in childbirth in 1817, and at the time was the only legitimate grandchild of King George?

10. Which blood disease was King George said to suffer from, and passed on to several of his descendants?
11. Who wrote the Foreword to John Brooke's biography of King George, published in 1972?
12. Who was King George's last surviving child, who died in 1857?

48. King George IV

1. Which of Prince George's mistresses was known as 'Perdita', after the role she had played on stage in Shakespeare's The Winter's Tale when he first saw her?
2. Which Catholic widow did Prince George marry illegally in 1785?
3. Which residence was commissioned by and built as a seaside retreat for the Prince Regent?
4. Which caricaturist drew the famous satirical cartoon, 'A Voluptuary Under The Horrors of Digestion' of Prince George in 1792?
5. Whose art collection did King George IV ask the government to purchase, in order that the paintings would form the nucleus of the National Gallery in London?
6. To which measure did the Duke of Wellington obtain King George IV's consent in January 1829 and become law three months later?
7. What did the Prince Regent allegedly ask the Earl of Malmesbury for after being introduced to his future wife Princess Caroline for the first time, saying that he was not well?
8. Which Prime Minister was assassinated in 1812 during the regency?

9. Which bill was introduced in Parliament in 1820 in an attempt to dissolve the marriage between King George and Queen Caroline?

10. Which famous writer was responsible for organising the King's visit to Edinburgh in 1821?

11. Which treaty did the Prince Regent ratify in December 1814, ending the war of 1812 between Britain and the United States?

12. Where in London did the Prince Regent hold a fete in June 1811 to celebrate the start of the regency?

49. King William IV

1. In 1789 Prince William was created Duke of Clarence and St Andrews, but which earldom was conferred on him at the same time?
2. At which naval battle of 1780 was he present as a midshipman?
3. Complete the following quotation which he made in the House of Lords on the issue of the slave trade: 'The proponents of the abolition are either fanatics or hypocrites, and in one of those classes I rank ...'
4. Which actress was the mistress of Prince William and bore him ten children?
5. Of which German duchy was William's wife Adelaide originally a princess?
6. When the King invited guests to dinner at the Royal Pavilion in Brighton, he told them not to 'bother about clothes' as the Queen did nothing but what after the meal?
7. Who was the King's Prime Minister at the time of the Great Reform Bill?
8. Which of the King's brothers was Viceroy of Hanover throughout his reign, as he had been during that of King George IV?
9. To which post was Prince William appointed in 1827?
10. When the King knew he was dying in June 1837, he asked his doctor to 'tinker' him up so that he might live to see another anniversary of which important event?

11. Which of the King's illegitimate daughters died in childbirth in April 1837, two months before he did, and whose death possibly contributed towards hastening his own?

12. The King was succeeded on the British throne by Queen Victoria, but who would be his successor as King of Hanover?

50. Queen Victoria

1840

1. In which year were Queen Victoria and Prince Albert married?
2. What was the name of her favourite Highland servant or ghillie, who died in 1883? *John Brown* ✓
3. The Victoria Cross was introduced in 1856, initially for acts of valour 'in the face of the enemy' during which war? *Crimean War* ✓
4. Which of the Queen's children was married in July 1862 in the dining room at Osborne House? *Alice* ✓
5. Where did the Queen live for the first eighteen years of her life until she ascended the throne? *Kensington* ✓
6. Victoria was her second Christian name. What was the first, given to her after one of the allied heads of state in Europe? *Alexandrina* ✓
7. Which imperial title was conferred on the Queen by the Royal Titles Act of 1876 and proclaimed at the Delhi Durbar on 1 January 1877? *Empress of India* ✓

Countess of Balmoral

8. When the Queen visited Florence on holiday, under which alias did normally she travel?

Ireland

9. Which country did Queen Victoria visit in April 1900, for the first time since before the death of the Prince Consort? *Coburg Germany* ✗
10. Which was the only one of the Queen's Prime Ministers who was born during her reign? *Earl of Rosebery*

11. Which of the Queen's children suffered from haemophilia and died while on holiday in Cannes at the age of thirty?

12. What did Edward Oxford, William Hamilton, Robert Pate and Roderick Maclean all have in common with relation to the Queen?

51. King Edward VII

1. In 1852 the young Edward's tutor Henry Birch left and was succeeded by which former barrister?
2. At which Cambridge college did Edward become a student in 1861?
3. At which cathedral was the first meeting between Edward and Princess Alexandra of Denmark arranged in September 1861?
4. Which European capital did Edward visit in September 1888, only to be asked to leave forthwith as the German Emperor William II was also going to be there and did not want him to be present at the same time?
5. At which house in Yorkshire was Edward among the guests when Sir William Gordon-Cumming was allegedly caught cheating at a game of baccarat?
6. When Edward visited Birmingham in November 1874, which mayor with supposedly republican sympathies and future senior minister greeted him?
7. At whose funeral in May 1898 was Edward one of the pallbearers, much to the annoyance of Queen Victoria?
8. King Edward's coronation was postponed from 26 June 1902 when he underwent an emergency medical operation that same week. On what date was the ceremony held later that summer?

9. Which President of the French Republic welcomed King Edward VII on his very successful visit to Paris in May 1903?

10. Who was the eldest daughter of King Edward VII, created Princess Royal in 1905?

11. In which year did King Edward VII and Queen Alexandra pay a long-delayed state visit to Berlin?

12. What was the name of the King's horse which won a race at Kempton Park in May 1910 on the afternoon of his death?

52. Queen Victoria's children

Excluding King Edward VII, who has a round of questions to himself above:

1. Which Fenian sympathiser attempted to assassinate Alfred, Duke of Edinburgh, while he was in Sydney on a tour of Australia in March 1868?
2. What was the name of the country house near Kronberg which the Empress Frederick had built in 1894 after the death of her husband, and where she lived until her death in August 1901?
3. At which house in Windsor Great Park did Prince and Princess Christian of Schleswig-Holstein spend most of their married life together?
4. Prince Arthur shared a birthday with which of his godfathers, a noted military commander and subsequently Prime Minister, after whom he was named?
5. Who was the controversial German theologian befriended by Alice, Grand Duchess of Hesse, in her later years?
6. Prince Leopold, Duke of Albany, was the great-grandfather of which European monarch, who ascended his throne in 1973?
7. The last formal engagement undertaken by Arthur, Duke of Connaught, was when he

opened the Connaught Gardens, which were named after him, in 1934 – in which English town?

8. What *faux pas* did Princess Beatrice accidentally commit at the coronation of King Edward VII?

9. Where in England were the German Crown Prince and Princess Frederick William staying in June 1878 when they were brought news of the attempted assassination and severe wounding of Emperor William I in Berlin?

10. On 24 May 1881, Prince Leopold was made Duke of Albany, Earl of Clarence, and which other title was conferred on him at the same time?

11. Although he was unable to accept the crown for political reasons, to which vacant European throne was Prince Alfred elected in a plebiscite in 1862?

12. For health reasons, where did Princess Louise spend Christmas 1883?

53. King George V

1. On which ship did Prince George and his elder brother Prince Albert Victor sail on three journeys around much of the world during their early days in the royal navy?
2. George, Duke of York proposed to Princess May of Teck while staying at the home of his sister Louise, Duchess of Fife and her husband – where?
3. Which imperial capital did King George V and Queen Mary visit in late 1911 for the Coronation Durbar?
4. Which journalist was prosecuted and imprisoned for libel in 1911 after claiming in a newspaper article that the King was a bigamist with three children from a marriage which he had contracted in 1890 in Malta?
5. According to his biographer Harold Nicolson, while he was Duke of York, Prince George was said to do nothing but shoot animals and what other activity?
6. Which sculptor designed the head of the King for the coronation medal and the coinage used throughout his reign?
7. Who was the youngest child of King George V and Queen Mary, who died at the age of thirteen?
8. Where was the King injured in October 1915 during the First World War, after his horse threw him and fell on him when he was reviewing his troops?

9. In 1922 the King ordered a ship to be sent to rescue members of which European royal family, one of whom was facing almost certain execution by firing squad?

10. Complete this sentence from the King's diary entry of 22 January 1924: 'Today 23 years ago dear Grandmama [Queen Victoria] died. I wonder what she would have thought of...'

11. Who was the unmarried sister of the King who died in December 1935, six weeks before him?

12. Which royal physician tended the King during his final illness?

54. King Edward VIII

1. At which castle in Wales did the investiture of Edward as Prince of Wales take place in July 1911?
2. Which naval establishment did he attend after leaving Osborne Naval College?
3. Which Secretary of State for War refused to allow him to serve on the front line during the First World War, because of the risk they would be taking if he was to be captured by the enemy?
4. Which military decoration was he awarded in 1916?
5. In which English town were the Assizes held in October 1936 at which the Simpsons' divorce case was heard and a decree nisi was granted?
6. Who addressed the Lambeth Conference on 1 December 1936, in which he rebuked the King for his lack of regular churchgoing?
7. Of which territory was the Duke of Windsor appointed governor during the Second World War?
8. On their visit to Germany in October 1937, who did the Duke and Duchess of Windsor meet and take tea with one afternoon at Berchtesgaden?
9. On which naval vessel were the Duke and Duchess brought from France to Britain in September 1939 by Earl Mountbatten of Burma?

10. Which American President did the Duke and Duchess visit at the White House in 1955?

11. For which physical problem was the Duke treated by Sir Stewart Duke-Elder in February 1965?

12. On which occasion did the Duke and Duchess appear in public alongside Queen Elizabeth II and Queen Elizabeth the Queen Mother on 7 June 1967?

55. King George VI

1. In which building on the Sandringham estate was Prince Albert born in 1895?
2. When Prince Albert became a midshipman in the Royal Navy in 1913, on which battleship did he serve?
3. In which sea battle in 1916 did Prince Albert take part?
4. Who was the speech and language therapist who successfully treated Prince Albert and helped him to master his stammer?
5. Who served as Private Secretary to the King from 1943 until the latter's death in 1952?
6. Which of the King's brothers was killed on active service in an accident in Scotland in August 1942?
7. Which body did the King address at its first assembly in January 1946 in London, at which he affirmed 'our faith in the equal rights of men and women and of nations great and small'?
8. Which Prime Minister of the Union of South Africa welcomed King George and Queen Elizabeth on their visit there in 1947?
9. Which President of the United States did King George VI meet on board ship off Plymouth in August 1945?
10. In which year did King George VI and Queen Elizabeth celebrate their silver wedding?

11. Which two countries was King George VI intending to visit in 1949, the tour being cancelled because of his ill-health?

12. Which surgeon removed the King's left lung during an operation in September 1951 after the discovery of a malignant tumour?

56. Queen Elizabeth II

1. Who was governess to Princesses Elizabeth and Margaret, later publishing a book of memoirs, much to the palace's disapproval?
2. Which year, according to a speech the Queen gave that December, was her 'annus horribilis' (or, as *The Sun* put it, 'one's bum year')?
3. After their wedding in 1947, which was the official London residence of the Duke and Duchess of Edinburgh until the latter's accession to the throne?
4. Who is the Queen's eldest grandchild, born in November 1977?
5. During the Silver Jubilee celebrations in 1977, the Queen presided at a banquet in London attended by the leaders of all members of the Commonwealth – how many were there altogether?
6. Which was the first of the Queen's Prime Ministers who was younger than her?
7. What surname was adopted in 1960 for the Queen's male-line descendants who do not have royal titles?
8. The Queen and the Duke of Edinburgh, both great-great-grandchildren of Queen Victoria, are second cousins once removed. Which European sovereign of the late nineteenth and early twentieth centuries is also an ancestor of both?

9. In 2008, where did the Queen attend the first Maundy service held outside England and Wales?

10. Who broke into the Queen's bedroom in Buckingham Palace in 1982?

11. In 1957, who was the editor of the *National and English Review* who wrote and published a controversial article in one issue, criticising the Queen's court for being too upper-class and British, and also the Queen's style of public speaking?

12. Which opening ceremony was performed in London by the Queen on 27 July 2012?

57. Scottish Kings and Queens

1. Who was the first King of Scotland, who founded the state in 843?
2. John, King from 1292 to 1296, was the only King of which house?
3. Which Scottish King was the first King of the House of Stuart?
4. In which year did the kingdoms of England and Scotland first share a monarch?
5. Which battle was fought between the English and Scottish in August 1542 during the reign of James V and resulted in a significant Scottish victory?
6. Where were Mary Queen of Scots and her father, King James V, born?
7. Who was the third husband of Mary, Queen of Scots?
8. Where was Mary Queen of Scots executed in 1587?
9. Which Dukedom was automatically conferred on the eldest son and heir of each Scottish King, and after falling into abeyance after the union of 1707, was revived in the reign of Queen Victoria to be used by her eldest son and heir apparent when in Scotland?
10. Which King granted the Incorporation of Surgeons and Barbers of Edinburgh a royal charter in 1506?

11. Margaret, Queen of Scots, who died in infancy in 1290, was also known as the Maid of Norway. Which Norwegian King was her father?

12. Which King, who reigned from 1040 to 1057, was immortalised as the title character in a play by William Shakespeare, although the drama is said to present a highly inaccurate picture of his reign and personality?

58. European Kings and Emperors

Turning to other countries, how well do you know European royalty from the nineteenth and twentieth centuries?

1. Which German Emperor was dying of throat cancer at his accession in 1888 and only reigned for three months, from March to June?
2. Where did Charles, former Emperor of Austria-Hungary, die in exile in 1922?
3. King Alexander I of Greece died in 1920 from blood poisoning after which tragic event?
4. Which monarch celebrated his diamond jubilee in 1908 and died in 1916 after a reign of sixty-seven years?
5. Carlota, or Charlotte to give her her original name, was the wife and consort of Emperor Maximilian of Mexico. She was born in 1840, the daughter of which European sovereign?
6. Victor Emmanuel II, who became first King of a united Italy in 1861, had previously become King of which territory in 1849?
7. Which Prussian sovereign appointed Otto von Bismarck to the Post of Minister-President in 1862?
8. When Norway declared its independence from Sweden, the monarch chosen to reign

over the Norwegians became King Haakon VII. Before that, he was Prince Charles of which country? DENMARK

9. Princess Anastasia of Montenegro's second husband was Commander-in-Chief of the Russian armies on the main front in the First World War – who was he?

10. Zog I was King of which country from 1928 to 1939? ALBANIA

11. Which King, who had been held in captivity for five years, was restored to the Spanish throne in 1813 as a result of the signing of the treaty of Valençay between Spain and France?

12. Leopold, Prince of Hohenzollern-Sigmaringen, who died in 1905, was the father of which early twentieth-century King?

59. Kings of France

1. Under the terms of the Treaty of Troyes in 1420, which French King recognized his son-in-law King Henry V of England as his Regent and heir?
2. Who was the first King of the house of Bourbon, reigning from 1589 to 1610?
3. Cardinal Richelieu was the chief minister of which seventeenth-century King?
4. Which King, who reigned from 1830 to 1848, was known as the Citizen King?
5. At which town were King Louis XVI and his family arrested in June 1791 when they tried to escape from Paris?
6. In 1572 King Charles IX permitted the killing of all Huguenot leaders who had gathered in Paris for the wedding of his sister Margaret of Valois to Henri of Navarre at the instigation of his mother Catherine de Medici. By what name is this deed remembered?
7. Which French King was the first husband of Mary, Queen of Scots, and therefore briefly King Consort of Scotland?
8. During whose reign was Joan of Arc burnt at the stake in 1431?
9. With which European power did King Louis XV sign the Treaty of Versailles in April 1756?
10. To which sovereign did Louis XII cede Naples at the Treaty of Granada in 1500?

11. Who was the second wife and Queen of King Francois I from 1530 to 1547, having previously been the Queen Consort of King Manuel of Portugal?

12. King Philip VI incurred the wrath of King Edward III of England when he provided refuge for which King of Scotland in France in 1334?

60. The Romanovs

1. Who was the first Tsar of Russia, elected in 1613? ALEXIS
2. Which Russian museum was founded by Catherine the Great in 1764 and was first opened to the public in 1852? HERMITAGE
3. The Great Northern War of 1700-21, during the reign of Peter the Great, was a war in which Russia contested the supremacy of which other European power? SWEDEN
4. At which treaty, signed in 1807, did Alexander I form an alliance with Napoleon Bonaparte?
5. Tsar Nicholas I died in 1855 during which conflict? CRIMEAN WAR
6. Which of Tsar Alexander II's sons was appointed General-Admiral of the Russian Navy in 1883?
7. Empress Marie Feodorovna, consort of Tsar Alexander III, was the daughter of which European King? CHRISTIAN OF DENMARK
8. Where was the coronation feast of 1896 held, in which over a thousand people were trampled to death?
9. Who was convicted and hanged for the assassination of Grand Duke Serge Alexandrovich in Moscow in 1905?
10. Which of Tsar Nicholas II's cousins was one of the conspirators implicated in the murder of Rasputin?

11. Which of Tsar Nicholas II's cousins claimed to be head of House of Romanov, and in effect Tsar of Russia, in 1924?

12. In which cathedral in St Petersburg were the remains of most of the Tsars laid to rest, including those of Tsar Nicholas II and his family in 1998?

61. Emperor Francis Joseph

1. Who was the uncle whom Francis Joseph succeeded as Emperor in 1848?
2. Who was the minister-president and foreign minister of Austria at the beginning of the Emperor's reign?
3. The Emperor married his cousin Elisabeth of Bavaria in 1854. Which of her sisters had the mothers of bride and groom originally planned for him to marry instead?
4. Which of the Emperor's younger brothers died in 1896 of typhoid after drinking water from the river Jordan?
5. How many times did the Emperor visit Great Britain?
6. At which hunting lodge did Crown Prince Rudolf take the lives of his mistress and then himself in January 1889?
7. Which Austrian territory was ceded to France, and then to Italy, by the terms of the Treaty of Prague after the Austro-Prussian War in 1866?
8. Which Hungarian nationalist attempted to assassinate the Emperor in February 1853?
9. The Emperor entered into the League of Three Emperors in 1873 with German Emperor William I and which other?
10. Which actress, whom the Emperor first met in 1885, became his mistress?

11. In October 1908 the Emperor announced the annexation of which two states into the Austro-Hungarian empire?

12. In which year did the Compromise or *Ausgleich* establish the dual monarchy of Austria-Hungary?

62. Emperor William II

1. Due to a difficult birth, the future Emperor had a withered hand and an arm shorter than the other – was it his left or his right?
2. Of the Emperor's three younger brothers, who was the only one who survived infancy?
3. Who was the Emperor's childhood tutor, appointed when he was about six years old?
4. What was the three-word title of Sir John Tenniel's cartoon which appeared in Punch after the resignation of Bismarck as Chancellor in March 1890, showing the Emperor looking down on him as he walked off the ship?
5. What relation was the Emperor to Queen Victoria?
6. Who was the British doctor summoned to treat his father Crown Prince Frederick William when he became ill in 1887?
7. At which port did the Emperor give his notorious speech in July 1900, addressing German troops who were leaving for China to suppress the Boxer rebellion, and mentioning Attila and the Huns?
8. Which town on the coast of Morocco did the Emperor visit in 1905, making a speech including remarks in favour of Moroccan independence, which led to friction with France?
9. What was the secret mutual defence agreement signed by the Emperor and Tsar

Nicholas II in July 1905 without the knowledge of their ministers, and to their horror?

10. After the dismissal of Hohenlohe as Chancellor in 1900, who did the Emperor appoint to the post, calling him 'his own Bismarck'?

11. After the Emperor abdicated in 1918 and was exiled to the Netherlands, he initially lived at Amerongen. Which house did he buy and move into in 1920 for the rest of his life?

12. After the Emperor's first wife, Empress Augusta Victoria, died in 1921, who did he marry the following year?

63. The Battenbergs and Mountbattens

1. What was the maiden name of the Princess of Battenberg, who was lady-in-waiting to Tsarena Marie Alexandrovna of Russia and married Prince Alexander of Hesse and the Rhine in 1851?
2. Who did Princess Marie, born in 1852, the first child of the marriage of the Prince and Princess of Battenberg, marry in 1871?
3. Which flagship of the North American and West Indies Station did their eldest son Prince Louis join in June 1869?
4. Which castle, near Jugenheim, was the main family home of the Battenbergs?
5. Who did Prince Louis succeed as First Sea Lord in December 1912?
6. Which peerage was bestowed on Prince Louis by King George V in November 1917?
7. Of which territory was Prince Alexander, the second Battenberg son, created Sovereign Prince in 1879 after the Treaty of Berlin?
8. Which princess would Alexander probably have married, had it not been for the opposition of the German Emperor William, several members of his family, and Chancellor Bismarck?
9. Who was the only daughter of Prince Henry of Battenberg and Princess Beatrice?

10. At which church on the Isle of Wight were Princess Beatrice and Prince Henry married in 1885 and also buried?

11. Which European sovereign unsuccessfully proposed in 1909 to Princess Louise, younger daughter of Prince Louis and later Queen of Sweden?

12. Which house near Romsey, Hampshire, was formerly the home of Lord Palmerston, and later of Earl Mountbatten of Burma and his family?

64. Who's on the cover

The cover shows portraits of twelve crowned heads, nine English and three European. (Admittedly, the first is more of an iconic representation which was painted long after the subject was dead, rather than a truthful portrait, but we'll let that pass).

Reading from top to bottom on each row in turn, they are shown in chronological order of birth. Can you name them?

65. Lucky Dip 5

I've started so I'll finish – no, I'll finish as I started – with one more general round:

1. In 1984, who became the first member of the royal family to appear in an episode of The Archers on BBC Radio 4?
2. With which principality is the House of Grimaldi associated?
3. Who was the mother of James, Duke of Monmouth, the illegitimate son of King Charles II?
4. What is the name of the summer palace in Corfu which was built for Elizabeth, Empress of Austria, and purchased in 1907 by the German Emperor William II?
5. Prior to his accession, in the fourteenth century which King of France was the first to hold the title of Dauphin as heir to the throne?
6. Who was Supreme Allied Commander, South East Asia Command, from 1943 to 1946, last Viceroy of India in 1947, and first Governor-General of the independent Dominion of India from 1947 to 1948?
7. On which Mediterranean island did Queen Victoria of Sweden frequently spend several months in autumn and winter for health reasons?
8. What was the name of the film production company of Edward, Earl of Wessex?

9. Which son of King George III specified in his will that he did not wish to have a state funeral, and was therefore buried in Kensal Green Cemetery?

10. Which house in Surrey was successively home to Princess Charlotte of Wales, daughter of the Prince Regent, and her husband Prince Leopold, and then ex-King Louis-Philippe of France?

11. Who was the last surviving grandson of Queen Victoria?

12. Richard, 1st Earl of Cornwall, Count of Poitou, and King of the Romans, was the younger brother of which King of England?

13. Including Princess Anne, how many princesses have held the style of Princess Royal since it first came into existence in 1642?

14. King Alexander of Greece died on 25 October 1920, the same day as which other member of the royal family who had close connections to Queen Victoria?

15. At which country seat in Hertfordshire did King James VI and I die in 1625?

16. Of which Holy Roman Emperor did Marcantonio Contarini write in 1536 that he was 'not greedy of territory, but most greedy of peace and quiet'?

17. Which Queen Consort, of a kingdom in eastern Europe, wrote poems, plays and novels under the pseudonym Carmen Sylva?

18. Which architect converted the Lady Chapel at the east end of St George's Chapel, Windsor Castle, into the Albert Memorial Chapel, between 1863 and 1875?

19. Which member of the royal family, a brother-in-law of the King at the time, died of

pleurisy in Egypt in January 1912, shortly after he was shipwrecked with his family off the coat of Morocco?

20. Which monarch is commemorated by an equestrian statue by Sir Francis Chantrey in Trafalgar Square, unveiled in 1843?

21. Which future British Queen Consort was born in the Yellow Palace, Copenhagen, on 1 December 1844?

22. Who was the father of Anne, Consort of King Richard III?

23. Who married Princess Stephanie of Belgium in Vienna in May 1881?

24. Which Austrian artist, born in Vienna, became the semi-official portrait painter to the courts of Britain and Germany, shortly after the death of Franz Xaver Winterhalter in 1873?

25. Who went out with her sister to mingle with the crowds in central London on Victory in Europe Day in 1945, and in a rare interview later said, 'I remember lines of unknown people linking arms and walking down Whitehall, all of us just swept along on a tide of happiness and relief'?

ANSWERS

1. Lucky Dip 1

1. Buckingham Palace
2. King George III
3. Catherine Parr
4. King William II (Rufus)
5. King William III
6. King Henry V
7. Russia
8. Bowes-Lyon
9. King Edward II
10. Nero
11. King John
12. Queen Marie Antoinette, Consort of King Louis XVI of France
13. King Charles I
14. King Richard I
15. King Henry VI
16. Queen Mary
17. King George I
18. Gloucester
19. King Alfonso XIII
20. King Henry III
21. Britannia
22. Queen Mary I
23. Tony Blair

24. King Henry VIII
25. September 2015

2. Browsing in the biographies

1. King Richard III
2. Princess Sophia, daughter of King George III
3. George, Duke of Cambridge
4. Albert, Prince Consort
5. Elisabeth, Empress of Austria
6. Queen Alexandra
7. Ludwig II, King of Bavaria
8. Rudolf, Crown Prince of Austria-Hungary
9. Elizabeth, Grand Duchess Sergei of Russia
10. Marie, Queen of Roumania
11. Princess Beatrice, formerly Princess Henry of Battenberg
12. Paul, King of Greece

3. So here it is, Royal Christmas, everybody's having fun

1. King William I
2. Queen Charlotte, Consort of King George III

3. 1932
4. Rudyard Kipling
5. Princess Alexandra of Kent
6. Osborne House
7. Minnie Haskins
8. Sandringham
9. 1957
10. *Twelfth Night*
11. King John
12. The coronation stone

4. Music

1. Mendelssohn
2. Elton John
3. Status Quo
4. Franz Ferdinand
5. Brian May
6. John Lennon
7. Queen Mary, wife of King William III
8. Arthur Sullivan
9. Princess Anne, later Princess Royal
10. The Electric Light Orchestra
11. Aix-la-Chapelle, or Aachen
12. Violin

5. Nicknames

1. King Harold I
2. King Henry I
3. King Richard I
4. King John
5. King Edward I
6. King Richard III
7. King Henry VIII
8. Anne of Cleves, briefly fourth Queen of King Henry VIII
9. King Charles II
10. Louis XIV, King of France
11. King George IV
12. King Edward VII

6. Death or glory – but certainly death

1. Queen Boudicca (Boadicea)
2. Valens I, Roman Emperor
3. Robert I, King of France
4. Brian Boru, King of Ireland
5. Harold Hardrada
6. King Harold II
7. Michael III of Bulgaria
8. John, King of Bohemia
9. King Richard III

10. James III, King of Scotland
11. James IV, King of Scotland
12. Charles XII, King of Sweden

7. An assassination has been announced

1. William I, Prince of Orange, 'William the Silent'
2. Henri III, King of France
3. Henri IV, King of France
4. Gustav III, King of Sweden
5. Alexander II, Tsar of Russia
6. Elisabeth, Empress of Austria
7. Umberto I, King of Italy
8. Peter and Draga, King and Queen of Serbia
9. Carlos I, King of Portugal, and his son and heir Crown Prince Luis Filipe
10. George I, King of Greece
11. Francis Ferdinand, Archduke of Austria-Hungary, and his wife Sophie, Princess of Hohenberg
12. Alexander, King of Yugoslavia

8. Good book, Your Majesty (or Your Highness)

1. King Henry VIII
2. William II, German Emperor
3. Stephanie, Crown Princess of Austria
4. Princess Beatrice, formerly Princess Henry of Battenberg
5. Princess Marie Louise
6. Queen Alexandra of Yugoslavia
7. Wallis Simpson, Duchess of Windsor
8. Charles, Prince of Wales
9. George, Earl of Harewood
10. Philip, Duke of Edinburgh
11. Princess Michael of Kent
12. Sarah, Duchess of York

9. Treading the boards

1. King Henry VIII
2. Queen Elizabeth I
3. King George III
4. The Prince Regent, later King George IV
5. Queen Victoria
6. Albert, Prince Consort
7. Victoria, Princess Royal, later German Empress Frederick
8. King Edward VII
9. William II, German Emperor

10. King George V
11. Nicholas II, Tsar of Russia
12. King George VI

10. Palaces, Residences and Abbeys

1. King George IV
2. Fontevrault
3. Buckingham Palace
4. King George II
5. Linlithgow
6. The Prince of Wales, later King Edward VII
7. Palace des Tuileries
8. Richmond
9. Osborne House
10. Sir Edwin Lutyens
11. Fort Belvedere
12. Livadia

11. The truth, the whole truth – or maybe not

1. True
2. False (He was executed in Mexico, but his body was returned to Vienna for burial)

3. True
4. True
5. False (His brother King James II was)
6. False (He never travelled overseas, and never even went north of Worcester)
7. True
8. False (He narrowly missed a would-be assassin's bullet in Brussels, not in Berlin, in 1900)
9. False (101 was a record royal age at the time she died, but in 2003 the Duchess of Gloucester, also born in 1900, died at 102)
10. True
11. True
12. False (She did demand to be admitted to the Abbey, but was sent away and gave up the struggle)

12. Lucky Dip 2

1. King Henry VI
2. King William IV (which means he is therefore descended from several, but this is the answer being looked for)
3. Belgium
4. Victoria Melita of Edinburgh, later Grand Duchess of Hesse and the Rhine, later Grand Duchess Kyril of Russia, and daughter of Alfred, Duke of Edinburgh
5. Newfoundland
6. Oscar Wilde
7. Diego Velazquez

8. Eleanor of Provence, Queen Consort of King Henry III
9. King Stephen
10. William II, German Emperor
11. Leicester
12. King Edward II
13. Kenya
14. Grimaldi
15. George, Duke of Clarence
16. *Lord of the Rings*, J.R.R. Tolkien
17. William, Duke of Gloucester
18. Canute (or Cnut)
19. The Netherlands
20. Philip, Duke of Edinburgh
21. Great-grandson
22. King Alexander
23. Carol I, King of Roumania Ferdinand
24. King William IV
25. Henry Stuart, Lord Darnley, second husband of Mary, Queen of Scots

13. Royal food

1. Victoria sponge
2. Coronation chicken – for Queen Elizabeth II's Coronation in 1953
3. Queen Elizabeth I
4. Marie Alexandrovna, Grand Duchess of Russia, to Alfred, Duke of Edinburgh
5. King Edward potato, introduced in 1902 at around the time of the King's coronation
6. Queen Margharita of Italy

7. The Prince of Wales, later King Edward VII
8. Gin (30%) and Dubonnet (70%)
9. Battenberg cake (which somehow survived the general renaming by King George V when his Battenberg relatives all became Mountbatten instead)
10. King George IV (who died less than three months later)
11. Waitrose
12. Charles Elmé Francatelli

14. A bit on the side

1. Nicholas II, Tsar of Russia
2. King James II
3. King Edward IV
4. King Edward VII
5. King George II
6. King William IV
7. King Edward VIII
8. Frederik VII, King of Denmark
9. King George IV
10. King Edward III
11. King Charles II
12. King Henry II

15. Now for the novels and plays

1. King Edward VIII, as prince
2. Elizabeth Woodville, Consort of King Edward IV
3. King William IV
4. Queen Matilda, consort of William the Conqueror
5. King Richard III
6. Louise, Duchess of Argyll
7. Queen Isabella, consort of King Edward II
8. Queen Elizabeth I
9. Princess Elizabeth of Hesse, later Grand Duchess Serge Alexandrovich
10. King Charles II, as prince
11. Jane Seymour, third consort of King Henry VIII
12. Queen Caroline, consort of King George II
13. Christopher Marlowe
14. Gordon Daviot (pseudonym of Elizabeth Macintosh, who also wrote under the name Josephine Tey)
15. Laurence Housman
16. Royce Ryton
17. Nick Stafford
18. Stephen Poliakoff

16. Go on, quote me

1. King George V
2. King George II
3. Queen Elizabeth, Consort of King George VI
4. King Charles I
5. Queen Elizabeth II, on her twenty-first birthday
6. Queen Elizabeth I
7. King Edward VII
8. King Frederick II of Prussia (Frederick the Great)
9. Philip, Duke of Edinburgh
10. Queen Mary, Consort of King George V
11. William II, German Emperor
12. Wallis Simpson, Duchess of Windsor

17. Dates, dates and more dates

1. Egbert
2. Alfred ('the Great')
3. Athelstan
4. Hardicanute
5. Henry I
6. Edward I
7. Richard II

8. Henry VI
9. James II (James VII)
10. William IV
11. Edward VIII
12. George VI
13. John VI
14. Paul
15. Michael
16. Baudouin
17. Charles IV
18. Charles X
19. Frederick William III
20. Ludwig II
21. Alfonso XII
22. Ferdinand
23. Christian IV
24. Oscar II

18. Yes, Prime Minister

1. King Edward IV
2. King Henry VIII
3. King George III
4. Queen Elizabeth II
5. King Edward VI
6. King George V
7. Queen Victoria
8. King Edward VII
9. Queen Elizabeth I
10. King William IV
11. Queen Victoria
12. King George V

19. Dogs and other pets

1. King Henry VIII
2. A greyhound
3. Susan
4. Prince Charles and Princess Anne
5. King Victor Emmanuel II
6. A wire fox terrier
7. A Skye terrier
8. Harvey
9. An African grey parrot
10. A King Charles spaniel
11. A fox
12. A pet crocodile

20. A royal musical free-for-all

1. James Darren
2. *God Save the Queen*
3. *Killer Queen*
4. *The Royal Mile*
5. *I'm Henry VIII, I am*
6. The Scaffold
7. Tyrannosaurus Rex
8. *Dancing Queen*
9. The Kinks
10. The Move (on the album *Looking On*)

11. Boney M
12. *Richard III*

21. Abdications

1. King Milan
2. King Stanislaus II Augustus
3. Prince Alexander
4. Queen Wilhelmina
5. King James II
6. Tsar Nicholas II
7. King Juan Carlos
8. Emperor Charles
9. King Victor Amadeus
10. King Albert II
11. King Victor Emmanuel III
12. King Michael

22. Lucky Dip 3

1. The Merry Wives of Saxe-Coburg Gotha
2. Princess Andrew of Greece, mother of Philip, Duke of Edinburgh
3. King James VI and I
4. King William IV
5. Philip, Duke of Edinburgh
6. Sweden
7. Anthony Van Dyck

8. King Alfonso XIII and Queen Victoria Eugenie of Spain, in Madrid
9. 1976
10. Wantage
11. Jane Seymour
12. King Edward VII
13. Queen Berengaria, wife of King Richard I
14. King George II
15. Princess Elizabeth, now Queen Elizabeth II
16. King Henry III
17. Alexander, Earl of Athlone
18. Sir Norman Hartnell
19. Queen Alexandra
20. King William II (Rufus)
21. Henry, Cardinal York, younger brother of Prince Charles Edward ('Bonnie Prince Charlie')
22. Pembroke
23. She was a Roman Catholic
24. Sir Thomas Lawrence
25. Sandringham

23. Armed Forces

1. The Auxiliary Territorial Service
2. William IV
3. The Falklands War, 1982
4. George, Duke of Kent
5. Royal Naval College, Dartmouth
6. Grenadier Guards
7. Devonport

8. Louis, Earl Mountbatten of Burma
9. George, Duke of Cambridge
10. RAF Cranwell
11. Arthur, Duke of Connaught
12. British Expeditionary Force

24. Who and who, or whom, or what

1. King George II to Queen Caroline, as she was dying in 1737, when she told him he should marry again
2. Grand Duke Alexander of Russia to Empress Alexandra, early in 1917, shortly before the Russian revolution
3. King Charles II to King James II
4. King William IV to Prince Leopold of Saxe-Coburg Gotha, later King of the Belgians; the comment may have been made after the latter had become King
5. King George V to Kenneth Clark
6. King George VI to John Piper, about his wartime paintings of Windsor Castle
7. Queen Victoria about William Gladstone
8. Arthur Wellesley, Duke of Wellington, about King George IV
9. King Edward VII about Emperor William II
10. Otto von Bismarck on Victoria, Princess Royal, later Empress Frederick, on the occasion of her engagement to the future Emperor Frederick III

11. Princess Margaret, announcing in 1955 that she had decided not to marry Group Captain Peter Townsend
12. Emperor Francis Joseph of Austria-Hungary, on being brought the news of the assassinations of his heir Archduke Francis Ferdinand and his wife Sophie at Sarajevo in 1914

25. The big picture

1. *Mrs Brown*
2. *The Madness of King George*
3. *Mary Queen of Scots*
4. *The young Victoria*
5. *The other Boleyn girl*
6. *The Queen*
7. *Elizabeth and Essex*
8. *Nicholas and Alexandra*
9. *The King's Speech*
10. *Anne of a Thousand Days*
11. *Queen Christina*
12. *The Lion in Winter*

26. Another quotation round

1. Edward, Prince of Wales, later King Edward VIII, to Lord Kitchener at the War

Office, 1914, asking for a role in the front line during the First World War

2. Diana, Princess of Wales, to Martin Bashir, 1995, in an interview on the TV current affairs programme *Panorama*

3. Albert Edward, Prince of Wales, later King Edward VII, to Eugenie, Empress of the French, 1855, saying he and his sister Victoria would love to stay in France longer and was sure their parents would not miss them

4. Princess Margaret, Countess of Snowdon, on her children

5. The German Empress Victoria, later Empress Frederick, in a letter to Queen Victoria, 1888, shortly after her dying husband ascended the throne as Emperor Frederick III

6. King George V, when questioned about his attitude as a father

7. King William IV in a speech at his 71st birthday dinner, 1836

8. Anne, Princess Royal, on being confronted by yet another press photographer

9. Catherine the Great, Empress of Russia

10. Queen Elizabeth, Consort of King George VI, to a suggestion that their daughters Princesses Elizabeth and Margaret should be evacuated to Canada for the duration of the Second World War

11. Queen Elisabeth of Greece

12. Farouk I, King of Egypt

27. Politicians

1. Tony Benn, then usually known as Anthony Wedgwood Benn
2. William (Willie) Hamilton
3. Stanley Baldwin
4. Lord Melbourne
5. Harold Wilson
6. John Pym
7. Simon de Montfort
8. David Lloyd George
9. Hugh Dalton
10. Margaret Thatcher
11. Benjamin Disraeli, Earl of Beaconsfield
12. James (Jimmy) Thomas

28. A question of sport

1. Minoru
2. Richard 'Bay' Middleton
3. Dick Francis
4. German Emperor William II
5. The Prince of Wales, later King Edward VIII
6. Football
7. Prince Christian Victor of Schleswig-Holstein
8. Frederick, Prince of Wales
9. Albert, Duke of York, later King George VI

10. Dunfermline
11. Constantine II
12. Prince Frederick Charles of Prussia

29. Bagehot

1. George III
2. William III
3. Louis-Philippe of France
4. Anne
5. James II
6. Sophia of Hanover
7. James I
8. George I
9. George II
10. William IV
11. George IV
12. Victoria

30. Shakespeare

1. King John (from *King John*)
2. Queen Eleanor (from *King John*)
3. King Richard II (from *Richard II*)
4. John of Gaunt (from *Richard II*)
5. King Henry IV (from *Henry IV, Part I*)
6. King Henry V (from *Henry V*)
7. Queen Margaret (from *Henry VI, Part II*)

8. Richard, Duke of York (from *Henry VI, Part I*)
9. King Henry VI (from *Henry VI, Part II*)
10. King Richard III (from *Richard III*)
11. George, Duke of Clarence (from *Richard III*)
12. King Henry VIII (from *Henry VIII*)

31. 1066 And All That

1. William II
2. Henry I
3. Richard I
4. Henry III
5. Edward III
6. Henry VII
7. James I
8. Charles II
9. James II
10. George III
11. William IV
12. Edward VII

32. Farjeon's Kings and Queens

1. William I

2. Richard I
3. John
4. Edward I
5. Edward II
6. Henry V
7. Edward IV
8. Edward V
9. Mary
10. Elizabeth
11. Anne
12. George IV

33. Lucky Dip 4

1. Edgar Boehm
2. Princess Margaret, later Countess of Snowdon
3. Francis II
4. Arnold Machin
5. John II (70 years, 1858-1929)
6. Diana, Princess of Wales
7. Queen Victoria
8. General Francisco Franco
9. Queen Anne (the names they used in their correspondence)
10. Adelaide (after the wife of King William IV)
11. Brazil
12. Henry Moore
13. Milan of Serbia
14. The Great Seal
15. Thailand

16. Hans Holbein
17. King George III
18. The Danish
19. Daniel Craig
20. Richard III
21. Camden Place, Chislehurst
22. Mary, Princess Royal, Princess of Orange
23. King Henry VIII
24. Edward, the Black Prince
25. Isabella of Angoulême

34. The Normans

1. The New Forest
2. Edgar II, or Edgar the Atheling
3. Adeliza of Louvain, also sometimes known as Adelicia, Adela and Aleidis
4. Domesday Book
5. Robert Curthose
6. Lincoln
7. Winchester
8. Carlisle
9. Anselm
10. Theobald of Blois
11. Reading Abbey
12. Westminster, sometimes known as Wallingford

35. The Plantagenets

1. Thomas Becket
2. Alfonso XIII of Castile
3. Ireland
4. Ballans
5. Bordeaux
6. Abbey of Santa Maria la Real de Las Huelgas, Castile
7. Roger Mortimer
8. Sluys
9. Order of the Garter
10. Duke of Hereford
11. Pontefract Castle
12. Edward, Earl of Warwick

36. The Lancastrians

1. John of Gaunt
2. Richard le Scrope
3. Rouen
4. Troyes
5. Rene, King of Naples
6. Eric of Pomerania, sometimes known as King Eric XIII of Sweden
7. Eton College
8. Shrewsbury
9. 1437
10. Jack Cade
11. Thomas of Lancaster, Duke of Clarence

12. Tewkesbury

37. The Yorkists

1. Northampton
2. Lieutenant of France
3. Edmund, Earl of Rutland
4. Mortimer's Cross
5. John Neville, later Marquis of Montagu
6. Sir John Grey
7. Charles the Bold, Duke of Burgundy
8. Earl of March
9. Pecquigny
10. King James III
11. Thomas of Lancaster, Duke of Clarence
12. Henry Stafford, Duke of Buckingham

38. King Henry VII

1. Lady Margaret Beaufort
2. Rennes Cathedral
3. John de la Pole, 1st Earl of Lincoln
4. Pope Innocent VIII
5. Margaret, King Henry's daughter
6. Beaulieu Abbey
7. Joanna, widowed Queen of Naples
8. Medina del Campo
9. Charles Brandon, Duke of Suffolk

10. Jasper Tudor, Earl of Pembroke
11. John Morton
12. Star Chamber

39. King Henry VIII

1. Greenwich Palace
2. Chester
3. Elizabeth Blount
4. Francis I
5. Fidei Defensor
6. Arthur
7. Spurs
8. Thomas Cromwell
9. Anne Boleyn
10. Supremacy
11. King James IV
12. The *Mary Rose*

40. King Edward VI and Queen Mary I

1. Jane Seymour
2. Lady Jane Grey
3. Pinkiecleugh
4. Hunsdon House
5. Cardinal Reginald Pole
6. John Cheke
7. Winchester Cathedral

8. Thomas Cranmer
9. Calais
10. Sir Thomas Wyatt
11. Miles Coverdale
12. John Knox

41. Queen Elizabeth I

1. Anne Boleyn
2. The Old Palace, Hatfield
3. Catherine Chapernowne, Catherine ('Kat') Ashley after marriage
4. Henry, Earl of Arundel
5. Carlisle
6. Sir Walter Raleigh
7. Thomas Howard, Duke of Norfolk
8. Lord Robert Dudley
9. The Faerie Queene
10. Sir Christopher Hatton
11. Ireland
12. François, Duc d'Anjou and Alençon

42. King James I and King Charles I

1. Henry Stuart, Lord Darnley
2. Church of the Holy Rude, Stirling
3. Bohemia

4. George Villiers, 1st Duke of Buckingham
5. 1617
6. The Popish Recusants Act
7. First cousin
8. Oxford
9. Henri IV, King of France
10. Ship money
11. On the grounds that a King cannot be tried by any jurisdiction on earth
12. Bedford House, Exeter

43. King Charles II and King James II

1. Duke of York
2. Declaration of Breda
3. Act of Uniformity
4. Secret Treaty of Dover
5. Edward Hyde, Earl of Clarendon
6. The Rye House Plot
7. The Cabak
8. Archibald Campbell, Earl of Argyll
9. Lowestoft
10. Holyroodhouse Palace, Edinburgh
11. Archibald Campbell, Earl of Argyll
12. Barbara Palmer, Duchess of Cleveland and Countess of Castlemaine

44. King William III, Queen Mary II and Queen Anne

1. Brixham
2. The Convention Parliament
3. Henry Compton, Bishop of London
4. Ryswick
5. 1694
6. John Graham of Claverhouse, Viscount Dundee
7. Limerick
8. George, Prince of Denmark
9. John Churchill, Duke of Marlborough
10. John Fenwick
11. Scottish Militia Bill
12. The Boyne

45. King George I

1. Act of Settlement
2. Order of the Garter
3. 1698
4. Leine Castle, or Leineschloss. His remains were moved to the chapel at Herrenhausen after World War II
5. Count Philipp von Königsmarck

6. Crown Prince Frederick William of Prussia, later King Frederick William I
7. False – contrary to popular legend, he could speak a little English, but not fluently
8. John Erskine, Earl of Mar
9. Septennial Act
10. Sir Charles Spencer, 3rd Earl of Sunderland
11. The South Sea bubble
12. Order of the Bath

46. King George II

1. Oudenarde
2. Monsieur de Busch
3. Ernest Augustus, Prince-Bishop of Osnabrück
4. Drury Lane Theatre
5. Thomas Pelham-Holles, 1st Duke of Newcastle
6. William, Duke of Cumberland, second son of King George II
7. Henrietta Howard
8. Dr John Ranby
9. Dettingen
10. Prince Frederick, who became King Frederick V of Denmark and Norway in 1746
11. William IV, Prince of Orange (to Anne, Princess Royal)
12. William Hogarth

47. King George III

1. Thomas Secker
2. Duke of Edinburgh
3. Margaret Nicholson
4. Royal Marriages Act
5. Princess Amelia
6. William Herschel
7. Weymouth
8. King of France
9. Princess Charlotte of Wales
10. Porphyria
11. Charles, Prince of Wales
12. Mary, Duchess of Gloucester

48. King George IV

1. Mary Robinson
2. Maria Fitzherbert
3. Royal Pavilion, Brighton
4. James Gillray
5. Sir John Julius Angerstein
6. Catholic Emancipation Act
7. A glass of brandy
8. Spencer Perceval
9. The Bill of Pains and Penalties
10. Sir Walter Scott
11. Treaty of Ghent
12. Carlton House

49. King William IV

1. Munster
2. Cape St Vincent
3. Mr (William) Wilberforce
4. Dorothy Jordan
5. Saxe-Meiningen
6. Embroider flowers
7. Charles Grey, 2nd Earl Grey
8. Adolphus, Duke of Cambridge
9. Lord High Admiral
10. The battle of Waterloo
11. Sophia, Lady de l'Isle and Dudley
12. Ernest, Duke of Cumberland, as King Ernest

50. Queen Victoria

1. 1840
2. John Brown
3. Crimean War
4. Princess Alice
5. Kensington Palace
6. Alexandrina
7. Empress of India
8. Countess of Balmoral
9. Ireland
10. Archibald Primrose, Earl of Rosebery
11. Prince Leopold, Duke of Clarence

12. They all attempted to shoot her

51. King Edward VII

1. Frederick Gibbs
2. Trinity
3. Speyer
4. Vienna
5. Tranby Croft
6. Joseph Chamberlain
7. William Ewart Gladstone
8. 9 August
9. Emile Loubet
10. Louise, Duchess of Fife
11. 1909
12. Witch of the Air

52. Queen Victoria's children

1. James O'Farrell
2. Friedrichshof
3. Cumberland Lodge
4. Arthur, Duke of Wellington
5. David Friedrich Strauss
6. Carl XVI Gustav, King of Sweden
7. Sidmouth
8. She noisily dropped her service book from the royal gallery on to a table of gold plate
9. Hatfield House
10. Baron Arklow

11. Greece
12. Bermuda

53. King George V

1. HMS *Bacchante*
2. East Sheen Lodge, Richmond-on-Thames
3. Delhi
4. E.F. Mylius
5. Stick in stamps
6. E. Bertram Mackennal
7. Prince John
8. Labuissière, France
9. The royal family of Greece
10. A Labour government
11. Princess Victoria
12. Lord Dawson of Penn

54. King Edward VIII

1. Caernarvon
2. Royal Naval College, Dartmouth
3. Earl Kitchener
4. The Military Cross
5. Ipswich
6. Dr Walter Blunt, Bishop of Bradford
7. The Bahamas
8. Adolf Hitler

9. HMS *Kelly*
10. Dwight D. Eisenhower
11. A detached retina in the left eye
12. The unveiling at Marlborough House of a memorial plaque to Queen Mary on her birth centenary

55. King George VI

1. York Cottage
2. HMS *Collingwood*
3. Jutland
4. Lionel Logue
5. Alan Lascelles
6. George, Duke of Kent
7. The United Nations
8. Jan Smuts
9. Harry S. Truman
10. 1948
11. Australia and New Zealand
12. Clement Price Thomas

56. Queen Elizabeth II

1. Marion Crawford ('Crawfie')
2. 1992
3. Clarence House
4. Peter Phillips
5. 36

6. John Major
7. Mountbatten-Windsor
8. King Christian IX of Denmark
9. Church of Ireland St Patrick's Cathedral, Armagh
10. Michael Fagan
11. John Grigg, 2nd Baron Altrincham
12. The Summer Olympics

57. Scottish Kings and Queens

1. Kenneth McAlpin, or Kenneth I
2. Balliol
3. King Robert II
4. 1603
5. Hadden Rig
6. Linlithgow Palace
7. James Hepburn, 4th Earl of Bothwell
8. Fotheringay Castle
9. Rothesay
10. King James IV
11. King Eric II
12. Macbeth

58. European Kings and Emperors

1. Emperor Frederick III

2. Madeira
3. He was bitten by a pet monkey
4. Francis Joseph, Emperor of Austria-Hungary
5. Leopold I, King of the Belgians
6. Sardinia-Piedmont
7. King William I
8. Denmark
9. Grand Duke Nicholas Nicholaievich
10. Albania
11. King Ferdinand VII
12. King Carol I of Roumania

59. Kings of France

1. Charles VI
2. Henri IV
3. Louis XIII
4. Louis-Philippe
5. Varennes
6. St Bartholomew's Day Massacre
7. Francois II
8. Charles VII
9. Austria
10. Ferdinand II, King of Aragon
11. Eleanor of Austria or Castile
12. David II

60. The Romanovs

1. Michael
2. The Hermitage
3. Sweden
4. Tilsit
5. The Crimean War
6. Grand Duke Alexis Alexandrovich
7. Christian IX, King of Denmark
8. Khodynka (or Khodinsky) Meadow, or Field
9. Ivan Kalyayev
10. Grand Duke Dmitri Paulovich
11. Grand Duke Kyril Vladimirovich
12. Cathedral of St Peter and Paul

61. Emperor Francis Joseph

1. Emperor Ferdinand
2. Prince Felix Schwarzenberg
3. Helene
4. Karl Ludwig
5. None
6. Mayerling
7. Venetia
8. János Libényi
9. Tsar Alexander II of Russia
10. Katherine Schratt

11. Bosnia and Herzegovina
12. 1867

62. Emperor William II

1. Left
2. Prince Henry
3. Georg Hinzpeter
4. Dropping the Pilot
5. Grandson (and her first grandchild)
6. Sir Morell Mackenzie
7. Bremerhaven
8. Tangier
9. Treaty of Björkö
10. Bernhard von Bülow
11. Huis Doorn
12. Princess Hermine Reuss, the widowed Princess von Schönaich-Carolath

63. The Battenbergs and Mountbattens

1. Julie (or Julia) Hauke
2. Count Gustav of Erbach-Schönberg
3. HMS *Royal Alfred*
4. Heiligenberg
5. Sir Francis Bridgeman

6. Marquess of Milford Haven (also Earl of Medina and Viscount Alderney)
7. Bulgaria
8. Princess Victoria of Prussia
9. Princess Victoria Eugenie, later Queen of Spain
10. St Mildred's Church, Whippingham
11, King Manuel II of Portugal
12. Broadlands

64. Who's on the cover

1. King William I
2. King Richard II
3. King Edward IV
4. King Henry VIII
5. Queen Elizabeth I
6. King Charles II
7. King George III
8. King Louis XVI of France
9. Queen Victoria
10. Tsar Alexander III of Russia
11. German Emperor William II
12. King George VI

65. Lucky Dip 5

1. Princess Margaret, Countess of Snowdon
2. Monaco
3. Lucy Walter
4. Achilleion
5. Charles V
6. Earl Mountbatten of Burma
7. Capri
8. Ardent Productions
9. Augustus, Duke of Sussex
10. Claremont
11. Alexander, 1st Marquess of Carisbrooke
12. Henry III
13. 7
14. Grand Duchess Marie of Russia, formerly Duchess of Edinburgh and Duchess of Saxe-Coburg Gotha
15. Theobalds Palace (or Theobalds House)
16. Charles V
17. Queen Elizabeth of Roumania
18. George Gilbert Scott
19. Alexander Duff, 1st Duke of Fife, husband of Louise, Princess Royal
20. King George IV
21. Queen Alexandra
22. Richard Neville, Earl of Warwick
23. Rudolf, Crown Prince of Austria-Hungary
24. Heinrich von Angeli
25. Queen Elizabeth II

The author

John Van der Kiste has written over sixty books, including historical and royal biographies, works of local history, true crime, music, plays and fiction. He has reviewed records and books for various national, local and independent publications and websites, and is a contributor to the *Oxford Dictionary of National Biography*. He lives in Devon.

For a complete list of his other titles currently available, please visit Amazon.co.uk/Amazon.com